Start Your Own

PHOTOGRAPHY BUSINESS

Studio ♦ Freelance
Gallery ♦ Events

Additional titles in *Entrepreneur's* **Startup Series**

Start Your Own

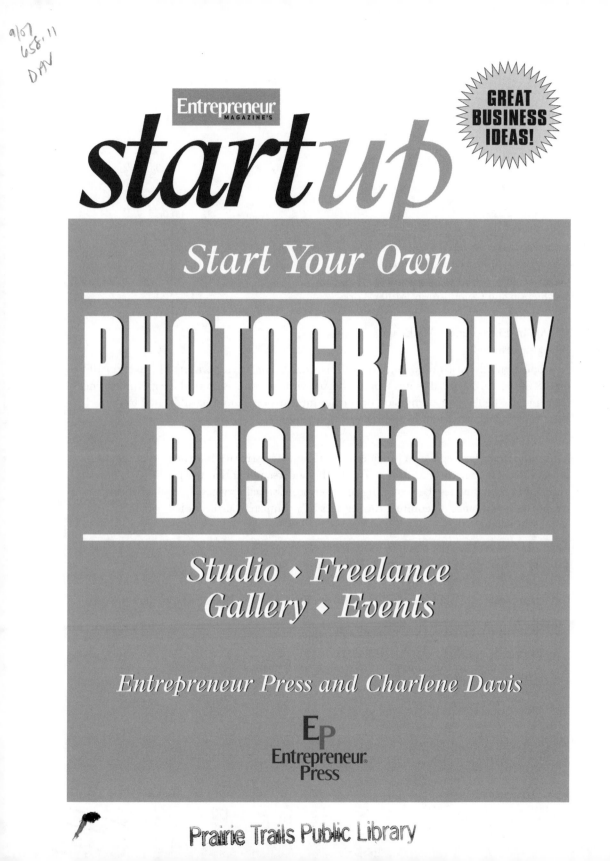

Entrepreneur
MAGAZINE'S

start up

GREAT
BUSINESS
IDEAS!

Start Your Own

PHOTOGRAPHY BUSINESS

Studio ◆ Freelance
Gallery ◆ Events

Entrepreneur Press and Charlene Davis

Ep
Entrepreneur.
Press

Editorial Director: Jere L. Calmes
Managing Editor: Marla Markman
Cover Design: Beth Hansen-Winter
Production and Composition: MillerWorks

This publication is designed to provide accurate and authoritative information in regard to the subject matter covered. It is sold with the understanding that the publisher is not engaged in rendering legal, accounting or other professional services. If legal advice or other expert assistance is required, the services of a competent professional person should be sought.

Library of Congress Cataloging-in-Publication Data
Davis, Charlene, 1957-
    Start your own photography business / by Entrepreneur Press and Charlene Davis.
    p. cm.
    ISBN-13: 978-1-59918-124-0 (alk. paper)
    ISBN-10: 1-59918-124-X (alk. paper)
    1. Photography—Business methods. I. Entrepreneur Press. II. Title.
TR581.D38 2007
770.68—dc22   2007024597

Printed in Canada

12 11 10 09 08 07   10 9 8 7 6 5 4 3 2 1

Contents

▲

Chapter 7

Business Structure: A Blueprint for Success. **51**

Chapter 8

Business Equipment for the Photographer **61**

Chapter 9

Help Wanted: Staffing Your Studio. **69**

Chapter 10

Marketing Made Easy. **77**

Chapter 14

Truisms: What You Won't See Through the Eye of the Camera

Preface

It has never been easier than now to turn an enjoyable hobby like photography into a lucrative, professional business. As the world's desire for panoramic moments steadily grows, so does the photography industry. New and interesting genres are constantly evolving and developing to keep up with society's need for better visual perspectives.

However, there are a number of responsibilities involved in operating a photography business and the purpose of this book is to help you streamline those tasks so that your

▲

business runs more smoothly and efficiently. While providing the information and tools to assist you in improving your performance as a professional photographer, we also want to emphasize the importance of operating sensibly and ethically.

One of the neat things about running your own business is that you are the boss (a/k/a head honcho, top dog, big cheese). The good news is that you get to make all of the decisions. The bad news is that you have to make all of the decisions. You also can't call in sick or defer to a higher authority. But don't worry, because we're going to help you get on top of your game with sage advice from successful professional photographers, strategies to market your business, nitty-gritty details about the photography industry, and much more.

This is a book for photographers, but it's not about photography—it's about setting up and running a photography business, whether from your home or in a commercial studio. We will provide you with the information you need to build and grow your business and to get on the fast track to success. So relax, start reading, and explore all of the options on how to build a profitable business in the wonderful world of photography.

1

The
Wonderful
World
of Photography

Many professional photographers start their careers as enthusiastic amateurs who discover they have a real talent for capturing creative images. Once they are bitten by the shutterbug, hobbyists immerse themselves in the world of picture making while investing hundreds (or thousands) of dollars on materials and equipment. To help defray the costs, amateurs sometimes sell their images to stock companies or use their artistic talents occasionally to photograph weddings and other events. This is when a hobbyist starts the crossover into the world of professional photography and finds it can be quite rewarding.

Starting a part-time or full-time career in photography is an excellent way to blend a passion with a steady income. Photographers can turn a fun hobby into a lucrative business that can easily be operated at home or in a commercial location. Of course, there is more to running a photography business than just snapping pictures.

A photography business can be a full-time operation with employees, or a part-time weekend venture that the entrepreneur can expand as desired. The business can be started with very little up-front cash, but there are a lot of considerations such as equipment (new or used), location for your darkroom or studio, supplies, and marketing, not to mention the traditional expenses associated with setting up an office and operating a business.

In this guide, you will find useful tips on how to set up a functional studio or darkroom, build a portfolio, learn about current trends in the industry, find paying jobs, understand the pros and cons of becoming an apprentice, and much more. We'll also discuss the advantages of participating in art shows and displaying your work in art galleries or other locales.

This book covers specialty areas such as weddings, portraits, events, fine arts, gallery, commercial, and digital imaging, and touches on photojournalism as well. It also discusses the difference between an assignment photographer and a stock photographer.

We offer suggestions on how to set up a fee structure in accordance with the type of services you provide. For example, a wedding package or family portrait sitting can generate a flat rate or an hourly fee, while stock pictures have a usage fee model. Plus, we explain the difference between royalty-free and rights-managed stock, and which method is better.

You also need to understand basic legal principals when taking photographs, including how to protect yourself from or prevent copyright infringement, when you should obtain consent so as not to violate privacy laws, and handling conflict and available remedies.

When you have your own business, you typically wear many hats and often more than one at a time. We'll help you discover the ones that "fit" the best by showing you how to design a photography business and studio that compliments your talents and your demographics.

Modern photography is as diverse as the bakery selections at Panera—and just as much fun to indulge in. But where the bakery goods can make you plump, photography can make you prosperous. Effectively pairing camera skills with business know-how can be one of the easiest and most rewarding ways to segue from an active hobbyist into a legitimate businessperson. What makes photography such an attractive career choice is the ability to ease into it as quickly or as leisurely as a person desires. This type of progression is one that few other occupations have. You don't see amateur physicians trying to do uncomfortable spinal taps or recreational lawyers representing complicated murder trials.

Photographers are far more likely to work for themselves than people in most other occupations, according to the *Occupational Outlook Handbook* put out by the U.S. Department of Labor's Bureau of Labor Statistics. Overall, the bureau counted some 129,000 people in the country who held jobs as photographers in 2004. Of these, more than half were self-employed, working in such specialty areas as portrait or wedding photography, advertising and product photography, and magazine photography. Photo studios doing portrait or commercial work, newspapers, magazines, and advertising agencies accounted for most of the salaried positions.

In the Beginning

While it is true that you learn things by doing, another way to learn is by example. After all, there's no reason you should repeat the mistakes of others if they're willing to tell you about them first. Throughout the book, you'll hear from our featured photographers who have started their own businesses. These folks built successful careers and have invaluable insight to share with you.

Let's start with **Michael Weschler,** a bicoastal lifestyle, celebrity, and commercial photographer who was known as "the kid with the camera" when he was just seven years old. Weschler loved taking pictures, but it never occurred to him that he might be an artist. "When I was young, I always equated being an artist with going mad like Van Gogh," he laughs.

It wasn't until his junior year in college that this architecture student discovered the magic that happens in a darkroom while taking a photography class. "After breezing through the class, I started doing street photography and fine art work on the side," Weschler says. "Then I switched my major to fine art and started taking drawing, sculpture, painting, and all of those disciplines." It was during the course of his studies that he rediscovered photography and decided to pursue it as a career.

Fun Fact

Today, women make up about half of all photographers, according to the web site of Professional Women Photographers (www.pwponline.org), an organization that formed in the 1970s when some female photographers decided there was a need for women to band together to "support each other in the male-dominated photography arena." While women have corrected the imbalance, the group continues to offer networking, advocacy, and other resources.

Part Time vs. Full Time

Many photographers—particularly home-based ones—start their business on a part-time basis and gradually move into a full-time operation. This process allows for more flexibility, especially if you want the other job to keep a steady cash flow coming while you establish your photography business. Also, if your current job offers a benefits package that includes insurance and retirement, that's another incentive to keep your homebased business a part-time operation. Starting part time gives you the opportunity to gain professional experience and build a solid reputation as a photographer. Some people continue working part time indefinitely until they retire or until they have built up enough cash reserve to sustain them during the first year's full-time operation.

"Initially I thought I was going to be a gallery guy and do fine art photography," he says. "But I was really torn with the whole art in commerce kind of dilemma and trying to find a balance."

Weschler says that it wasn't until he starting working with other photographers that he realized there was a place for him in commercial photography. "This was an area where I could create work for other people—as opposed to doing it for myself—and still feel like an artist," he says. Today, Weschler is a renowned lifestyle and celebrity photographer whose works have been featured in *GQ*, the *New York Times*, *Allure*, *Food & Wine*, *In Style*, and many other publications. He maintains homes, studios, and client bases in Los Angeles and New York City.

Ira Gostin of Reno, Nevada, had an early start in photojournalism at the age of 15. "I used to ride my bicycle to assignments for the little weekly newspaper where I grew up in Northern California," he relates. As his passion developed, he went on to study photojournalism at California State University, Long Beach, while working as an intern for the *L.A. Times*. With a foot already in the door, his photography career began with the *L.A. Times* and the Associated Press, covering world events—including the 1984 and 1988 Summer Olympics. Over time, he made the transition from photojournalism to corporate and advertising photography.

Gostin's unique style of visual storytelling has brought him nationwide acclaim as well as a Pulitzer Prize nomination. His work has been featured in almost every major newspaper and magazine in the world. A dynamic and inspiring speaker, he has taught photojournalism classes and delivered workshops across the country on photography, marketing, and customer service. Following his entrepreneurial spirit,

Gostin is currently enrolled in graduate school to earn an MBA in marketing so that he can move into the creative and marketing side of the business.

When he was just 12 years old, **Jerry Clement** of Winter Springs, Florida, shot his first wedding. "It wasn't anything elaborate, and all I had was an old Ansco box camera. But it was a great experience," he says. A few years later, he became the photographer for the high school yearbook, and after graduation, he maintained his interest in the photography field as an ongoing hobby. However, it wasn't until 30 years later when Clement retired as an insurance auditor that he decided to pursue his vision of becoming a professional photographer of fine art.

He has mastered the rare technique of processing Ilfochrome prints (f/k/a/ Cibachrome), which is still preferred by many art galleries and collectors because of its archival properties, not to mention its stunning clarity of colors. Today, Clement's beautiful fine art images are displayed in local galleries and grace the walls of residences and commercial offices of discerning art collectors.

Ray Strawbridge of Bunn, North Carolina, graduated from college in 1976 with an degree in broadcasting, journalism, and speech. He worked a few months as an audio-visual director before moving to his wife's hometown to help out with the family grocery business. Shortly thereafter, he opened a small studio in a nearby college town to do portraitures and framing—with minimal success. "My wife reminded me after a couple of years that I wasn't getting rich," he chuckles. "So, I started doing contract photography work with the local community college system."

Strawbridge closed his studio and worked on-site at campus laboratories, which eventually segued into more lucrative assignments. It wasn't until he started working for a log cabin company that he found his niche. "That's when I really got into architectural photography," he says. "I traveled up and down the East coast taking pictures of log cabin homes to be used in advertisements, planning guides, and magazine publications." Since then, Strawbridge has produced thousands of images for magazine covers, feature stories, annual reports, and advertisements, specializing in architectural, product, industrial, and food photography, as well as executive portraiture.

Once upon a time, **Carmen Davis** of Carnation, Washington, worked in the corporate world of human resources and frequent flyer miles. But after years of carving out health benefit plans and settling sexual harassment cases, she decided to leave that all behind to concentrate on her first love: Pharaoh Hounds. Davis has been breeding and showing champions for years, which allowed her to develop a keen eye and sharp instinct to know the precise

"I think..."

Famous Quote

"At 42, I decided to become a photographer because it offered a means of creative thought and action. I didn't rationalize this; I just felt it intuitively and followed my intuition, which I have never regretted."

—Wynn Bullock

moment these dogs were at their best on the lure course. "I've been involved with dogs for a long time," she says. "All of us who compete with our dogs are hungry for pictures, so that kind of started the idea percolating about getting involved with photography as a sideline. I figured at the very least it would pay for my camera and equipment."

Davis' theory proved to be a profitable one because she started collecting orders the first time she made an official appearance as a photographer at a dog show. This trend continued to this day, and Davis has expanded her business to include an online store with unique gifts, apparel, posters, prints, and more, all featuring pictures of canine athletes that can be custom ordered for the discriminating pet owner.

Looking Ahead

In an article published on ArtSchools.com, Eugene Mopsik, executive director of the American Society of Media Photographers (ASMP), says, "There are two facets to photography: the creative side and the business side." Mopsik recommends that serious photographers learn everything they can about the day-to-day procedures and cost of doing business, including budgeting and insurance. "You can be a great photographer," he adds. "But if you have poor business acumen, you might be in business for a while, but you'll be losing money."

To help you find your balance, we're going to start with an overview of the market, look at the specific services you'll want to consider offering, and then go through the step-by-step process of setting up and running your new venture. You'll learn about basic requirements and start-up costs, day-to-day operations, and what to do when things don't go according to plan. We'll discuss how to find, hire, and keep good employees. Plus, you'll gain a solid understanding of the sales and marketing process, as well as how to track and manage the financial side of your business.

What you won't learn is how to "get rich quick" or become an overnight success. Being a professional photographer requires hard work, dedication, and commitment. That's what running a business is about. You're going to love parts of the process and you're going to learn to like other parts; as for the rest—you're simply going to learn.

Make Things Click by Finding Your Niche

People enter the photography business from many different avenues. They may be career specialists looking for a change; students on the brink of new venture; hobbyists wanting to take a professional leap; or retirees ready to start a new chapter in life.

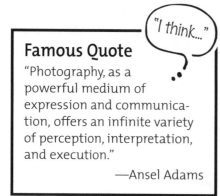

Before you can begin any serious business planning, you must first decide—at least tentatively—what type of photography you're interested in. As you consider the niche you want to get into, think about your own likes and dislikes, skills, and resources. For example, a photojournalist shoots spontaneously and has the uncanny ability to look through the viewfinder with one eye, while watching his surroundings with the other in anticipation of his next shot. On the other hand, a portrait photographer needs the patience of a saint and to enjoy the minutiae of the fussy staging process before capturing the perfect pose.

In this chapter, we look at some of the more common specialty areas and how one or two might work for you.

Photographer Specialty Areas

The field of photography is probably more diverse than most, and as there is an amazing amount of ground to cover, we're not going to attempt to include every area in this book. We'll just focus on a few specialties that seem to be of significant interest to many photographers, and hopefully to you.

Fine Art Photography

Fine art photography is for the creative individual who enjoys taking pictures for their aesthetic value—landscapes, nature, wildlife, nudes, or portraits. These high-quality images are often categorized as works of arts that are sometimes displayed and sold in galleries, with prints reproduced in limited editions for collectors, dealers, and curators. Gallery prints are a relatively new phenomenon because it wasn't until the 1970s that fine art photographs were deemed worthy of being shown alongside paintings, sculptures, and other objects d'art.

Although Jerry Clement does commissioned pieces on assignment when clients want specific images in a particular configuration, he says that most of his images are shot in advance. "I typically take pictures of things and places I enjoy," he says. "Then I do the best job I can to produce a pleasing image and hope that someone else will be interested in it as well."

Collectors also have a special interest in fine art photography books because they are usually limited editions with a short run and no reprints. Fine art images are sometimes printed on note cards, calendars, and posters, although some collectors would consider those to be "inferior" products. One wonders if Ansel Adams would agree.

Fine art photography is truly "in the eye of the beholder"—or camera. Some people think anything that is worthy of framing and hanging on a wall should be classified as fine art. But many artists would cringe at that interpretation. The question of whether photography is actually art has been disputed for decades, and it really comes down to:

1) its visual appeal,
2) the photographer's perception, and
3) the public's opinion.

Add those to a great marketing plan, and you're in business.

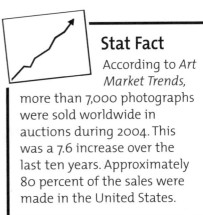

Stat Fact

According to *Art Market Trends,* more than 7,000 photographs were sold worldwide in auctions during 2004. This was a 7.6 increase over the last ten years. Approximately 80 percent of the sales were made in the United States.

Photojournalism

Photojournalism is the ability to tell a story through images of a particular subject or occasion. The photographer dons a "cloak of invisibility" and shoots the scenario before him or her without interfering in any way—in other words, no staged or formal shots.

"To be a photojournalist, you have to hustle," advises Ira Gostin. "It's not just about taking the best picture: it's about being more professional, more aggressive and pushing yourself. If that means climbing to the top of a building or a tree to get a better picture and tell a better story, then that's what you have to do."

The story is told through the eyes of the photographer as he sees it. Two people could be at the same place at the same time and make very different observations. An example would be standing on the bank of a river preserve near sunset. One photographer might capture the sun setting between the cypress trees over the water while the other would focus on the encroachment of a large housing development marring the landscape.

Editorial photojournalism is used in the presenting of news material and events, which means photographers are constantly on the move and need to make instantaneous decisions. This can sometimes be a risky business if the photographer is in the middle of a police standoff or shooting a natural disaster. And it can be heartrending when photographing scenes immediately following a tragedy.

The candid style of the photojournalist is also becoming very popular in commercial photography and is used regularly at events such as weddings or other social functions.

However photojournalism is used, there are certain elements that should always be present. Viewers must receive insight from the images. Images should be accurately portrayed in a chronological sequence of events. Also, photographers must use good judgment and objectivity so their pictures will be presented as an impartial narrative. In other words, the photojournalist must tell the truth as it naturally unfolds. If he attempts to manipulate the scene in any way—even something as simple as moving two people closer together—then the truth has been altered. So no Photoshop® doctoring.

Wedding Photography

Wedding photography is for the individual who enjoys working with people and wants to help them celebrate one of the most memorable days of their lives. Most of the work is done on location, although some photographers have studios for bridal portraits and engagement photos.

This may be surprising to some, but wedding photography is one of the most challenging areas of photography. The photographer has a very limited amount of time to take as many shots as possible of carefully arranged groups of people, while managing to make everyone smile and look beautiful—all at the same time. It really gets interesting when multiple location shots are desired and the weather conditions are inclement on this joyous occasion. A good photographer will not only be able to artfully capture these treasured moments, but he will also help the wedding party relax and have fun during this brief, hectic period. A grumpy photographer who is curt and short-tempered will not get many referrals, no matter how talented he is. People skills are a must.

For years, wedding photos have been carefully scripted poses of ring exchanges, cake cutting, and bouquet tossing. These formal, staged memories are still very much a part of the wedding album package; however, a new genre of wedding photography has emerged: wedding photojournalism. This is an approach to shooting the big day emphasizing a candid documentary style of photography. To help set the standards and advance the field, the Wedding Photojournalist Association (www.wpja.com) has stepped up to provide resources for "professional photographers skilled in the documentation of weddings and events in a candid, unobtrusive style." The group dates the style to the mid-20th century, when working photojournalists set the tone shooting high profile brides such as Grace Kelly and Marilyn Monroe.

The traditional, formal style will always be a mainstay for weddings, but that should not be the only style used. A wedding photographer should have his own unique, defined style that differentiates him from the throng of other wedding photographers. Today's bride is not going to be influenced by someone's superior lighting and posing capabilities—she wants originality.

Ray Strawbridge thinks some of the most successful photographers are those who do weddings

Bright Idea

Incorporate an artistic blend by shooting some photos in black and white; then hand color certain areas like the flowers. Try different lenses and filters for unusual results. Be creative!

and portraits. "As much as I hate to think of photography as a commodity, you have to find a service that people need or strongly desire," he says. "And regardless of what the economy is like—how much gas costs or who is unemployed—if there is a wedding, someone is going to take pictures." Strawbridge also feels this is one of the easiest niches to get started in. A photographer could start out by doing weddings on weekends and later add bridal portraits to the business. A natural offspring would be to include other types of portraiture such as children and families.

Portraiture

Portraiture is the art of recording people (and sometimes objects) at their best, be it through a painting, sculpture, or photograph. Portrait photography has become a wide-ranging commercialized area because so many people enjoy having portraits made to commemorate special events like family reunions, weddings, and graduations. Fortunately, portrait photography has come a long way since the old days of the

A Special Kind of Photographer

Children's photography is one of the fastest growing segments in portraiture, and there are many ways to narrow this field down to a finely tuned niche. Karen Dórame discovered this by accident in 2001 when she co-founded the Special Kids Photography of America (SKPA), a nonprofit organization that trains photographers to work with children who have special needs and disabilities. The organization was born out of Dórame's frustration of being unable to find a professional who was comfortable photographing her own special needs child.

"Statistics show that at least one in five children has some sort of disability or serious illness," Dórame points out in an interview with Lynne Eodice for Double Exposure. "This is over 20 percent of our population."

The organization has trained approximately 200 photographers nationwide how to work more effectively with special children, who can then use the SKPA name and logo in their marketing efforts when advertising.

Even if you are not planning to work specifically with special needs children in your niche, this type of training can still be invaluable. An example would be photographing a family reunion or wedding with a disabled child and being able to make everyone feel comfortable while taking some great shots.

To learn more about SKPA, visit www.specialkidsphotography.com.

daguerreotypes with the stern looking parents and grimmer-than-death children huddled around them.

Today's portrait photographers are no longer happy simply portraying someone's likeness on film in the traditional, posed style. They want to capture their subjects' personalities and stamp something of their essence onto the photograph. This is why a lot of portrait photographers go outside the studio and take photographs in natural settings, such as outdoors or in the home or business of the individual. Some photographers even have portable studios that include scenic backdrops and lighting equipment.

Bright Idea

Most portrait photographers agree that you need to get a good, rigid tripod to keep the camera stable, and a cable release that will allow you to click the shutter without ever touching the camera.

As a lifestyle photographer, Michael Weschler has produced a lot of celebrity portraits and enjoys combining his talent for shooting interiors with big personalities. "Clearly, these are not real moments, but I want to give viewers the feeling that these are real people in real settings," he says. For example, if someone is in their living room, Weschler is not going to have them wear an evening gown. Instead, you may see them playing with their dog, sitting at the piano, or just walking in from making an espresso in the kitchen. "I think there is a difference between creating a moment vs. contriving it and having it feel artificial. It's important to be as realistic as possible."

Smart Tip

Tip...

Americans' passion for pets has led to increased opportunities for photographers as pet photography has taken a prominent place in the $2.7 billion pet service industry, according to *The Deseret News,* a Utah newspaper. The trend got a further boost when it became a Hollywood craze, according to a 2007 article by Kelli Michael distributed by *Associated Content,* which reported that typical sitting fees range from $50 to $200, with photo packages priced at $200 to $1,000, depending upon location and clientele.

Photographers in the portraiture business have also learned what types of pictures sell best. For example, the picture of a frilly dressed three-year-old looking demurely down at her posies may be great for a calendar or poster, but her parents will most likely buy the close-up shot of her smiling, cherubic face. In group settings, the general preference is positioning men taller than the women—even if in reality the husbands are shorter than their wives.

In addition to arranging subjects to their best advantage, a portrait photographer also has to charm them into feeling their best. The more relaxed and comfortable they feel, the better the end results will be. This means a portrait photographer also has to be a people person. If you are more involved in how the lighting and equipment is set up than in how the individuals are responding, that attitude will bounce off your subjects and be reflected in the final images.

Event Photography

Event photography is pretty much self-descriptive. You are capturing events as they unfold at weddings, proms, political or sporting events, pet shows, school or business functions—basically wherever the action is. However, event photography is also a very broad term, and you should narrow down the field to include no more than two or three types of events that you specialize in. The more specialized your niche is, the better.

Although you will see and hear the terms "photojournalistic" and "documentary" used interchangeably in event photography, the two styles are quite different. The most prevalent style is documentary, which is a presentation of the facts that includes portraits, classic formals, and still life shots, along with candid moments. A photojournalistic style is the telling of a story through pictures, with no interference from or staged shots by the photographer.

Photographing an event can be a challenge. It's not always practical to use a flash and shooting in natural or ambient light can sometimes be tricky—it can be distracting or even prohibited at some events. You're also going to be moving around a lot, so travel lightly with only the essentials in your case (don't forget backup batteries). Wear dark clothing so that you can blend into the background and remain as inconspicuous as possible. You may also want to slide some wristbands on to keep sweat from trickling down your hands. Get as much information as you possibly can before attending the event to help you anticipate where you need to be and when.

Additional Photography Fields

Of course, these specialty fields by no means capture the vast world of photography in its entirety. Let's take quick look at some additional areas you may want to consider:

- *Advertising and commercial photography.* Photographers are typically employed full or part time by an agency or company to take pictures for ads, catalogs, brochures, newsletters, etc.

- *Scientific and technical photography.* Photographers need to understand and illustrate the subject she or he is photographing. The pictures can be used for research, presentations, education, and other purposes. Photographers are usually in-house and rarely freelance.

- *Architectural and industrial photography.* For the individual who appreciates structural design. Photographers must be skilled in taking both interior and exterior shots.

- *Forensic and evidence photography.* Photograph crime scenes and autopsies for scientists and law enforcement agencies.
- *Photographic analysis.* This field requires studying and analyzing images to determine if they have been altered or tampered with.
- *Public relations photography.* Photographers specifically hired to promote businesses or individuals by taking pictures at documented and prearranged events.
- *Sports photography.* A subset of event photography, it comes with the best seats in the house. With this adventure comes the danger of being squashed by a 250-pound linebacker while capturing the perfect catch on film.
- *Nature and wildlife photography.* It's perfect for someone who enjoys the outdoors and enjoys photographing animals, landscapes, and wildlife.
- *Underwater photography.* Photographers should be excellent swimmers with scuba diving skills and special underwater camera equipment.
- *Fashion photography.* Sort of a cross between commercial and portrait photography, photographs are used for magazines, ads, catalogs, and web sites.
- *Glamour photography.* A type of portrait photography, it's used to photograph people (usually women) at their best and most glamorous advantage.
- *Food photography.* Images made for restaurants, supermarkets, and food companies are used for promotion in posters, ads, circulars, magazines, and menus.
- *Aerial photography.* Images taken from the air (e.g., helicopter, plane, balloon, kite) are used for military purposes, commercial advertising, land use planning, environmental studies, etc.
- *Travel photography.* It's for individuals who enjoy being on the road, but it's very competitive.
- *Real estate photography.* Most of these pictures are used for high-end real estate properties, both residential and commercial.
- *Catalog photography.* It involves shooting specific product images, sometimes with special equipment and techniques.
- *Pet photography.* It's a great specialty for the photographer who knows and loves animals.
- *School photography.* This photography can be for class portraits, sports team photographs, teacher portraits, etc.
- *Portfolio photography.* Artists, corporations, models, and actors need photographs of their work or themselves for presentations.

The various fields of photography often complement and segue into another. Many photographers feel comfortable shooting in two or three specialties. If you look at the work of the photographers we have profiled in this book, you will notice most have more than one specialty area.

Market Research

Once you have chosen your niche or specialty, you will need to do an in-depth examination of your market. This assessment is essential to your success because it will provide you with information that helps you identify and reach your targeted audience as well as solve or avoid potential marketing problems. Ira Gostin strongly advises photographers to find out who their client base is. "Market research is absolutely the number one thing," he says. "It means getting on the phone and asking questions; find out who is doing what and what customers want."

Decide on the geographic area you want to serve and determine if you have enough people in that area who meet your customer profile. For instance, you may want to carve a niche in sports photography, but your area does not support any pro teams or large colleges and universities. In that case, you have two choices: you can either change the targeted geographic area or you can change your strategy to focus on youth leagues and local high school games while you gain some valuable experience. This also gives you an opportunity to build your portfolio and expand your network of contacts before communicating with the big boys at the wire services.

Conducting market research also gives you information about your competitors. You need to find out what they're doing and how that meets—or doesn't meet—the needs of the market. One of the most basic elements of effective marketing is differentiating yourself from the competition. One marketing consultant calls it "eliminating the competition" because if you set yourself apart by doing something no one else does, then you essentially have no competition.

However, before you can differentiate yourself, you first need to understand who your competitors are and why your customers might patronize them. Offering something no one else is offering could give you an edge in the market—but it could also mean that someone else has tried that and it didn't work. Don't make hasty decisions; do your homework before finalizing your services. Use the Photographer's Niche Worksheet on page 16 to help you define your target market.

Carmen Davis knew she had a targeted market shooting athletic dogs on the lure course. Thus, the name of her business: Dogs in Motion. "When shooting dogs, you have to know the precise millisecond when the animal is in the perfect position, because there are only two times in an entire stride of a running

Smart Tip

Tip...

Michael Weschler says that it's important to keep a balance and have some diversity as a photographer. "There is a danger in saying, 'I'm only going to do this specific type of work,' because you may have a dry spell. It might help to have something else going on, too."

Photographer's Niche Worksheet

How well have you defined your targeted market? This list can help you get organized and coordinate your efforts:

Identify three specialty areas you would like to target:

1. _____
   _____

2. _____
   _____

3. _____
   _____

What specific skills do you have in those areas?

_____
_____
_____
_____

Will you need additional training or education?

_____
_____
_____
_____

What additional equipment will you need?

_____
_____
_____
_____

Identify your clients:

_____
_____
_____
_____

What services do they need?

_____
_____
_____
_____

Who is your competition?

_____
_____
_____
_____

How will your services be different?

_____
_____
_____
_____

Is your geographical location favorable to your business?

_____
_____
_____
_____

dog that are picture worthy." This is why she recommends that photographers know their niche well.

Competition is keen in most places as increasing numbers of people are drawn to professional photography by such factors as the digital revolution. This makes the field more accessible. So does the growth of marketing opportunities brought about by the internet, as the Bureau of Labor Statistics notes. Still, the majority of photographers work in metropolitan areas. A search of the World Wide Web suggests that some areas are particularly packed with photographers. Cities such as Santa Fe, New Mexico; Portland, Oregon; and Missoula, Montana have all been touted in web postings as having more photographers per capita than anywhere else, as has Singapore. In a specialty niche, Salt Lake City, Utah, has both the most wedding photographers and the most weddings per capita, according to one Salt Lake City studio's web site.

Bright Idea

As the internet increases in popularity and usage, you'll find more and more of your competitors have web sites, which you can visit to find out what type of services they offer. Or you can simply call them, pretending to be a prospective customer, and ask about what they do, how they operate, and how much they charge.

3

Taking Stock
or Working
on Assignment

n the early-to-mid 1900s, stock photography images were basically leftovers from various commercial assignments, commonly referred to as "outtakes" or "seconds." Stock image libraries (now called "agencies") cataloged and published the images pretty much the same way any other

▲

product catalog did their merchandise and sold them for purchase and republication in ads, books, annual reports, etc.

As time passed, customers came to realize they could save considerable time and money by using stock images instead of hiring a photographer for a specific assignment. Stock agencies endeavored to meet the increasing demands by trying to foresee their customers' needs and communicating them to photographers. By the 1980s, stock photography had become a specialty in its own right, with many photographers enjoying the flexibility of shooting stock instead of working on assignment and receiving residual income (royalties).

Most of our featured photographers do both stock and assignment photography, although they usually prefer one over the other. Since you will probably work in both genres during your career, we thought we should give you some background on how they function.

Taking Stock

Stock images are everywhere you look: advertising, brochures, billboards, presentations, and web sites. Today, these images are regularly used by many commercial entities such as architectural and design firms, advertising agencies, publishers, magazines, and corporations, as well as web designers and graphic artists.

How It Works

During the 1980s, photographers controlled the rights for their images. Then in the new millennium, royalty-free images with unlimited usage rights were introduced through large stock agencies. In today's market, stock photographers are faced with the struggle of accepting a flat royalty-free fee or fight to retain royalty control rights of their images. Unfortunately, the battle is weighing heavily on the royalty-free side. This newer model is slowly replacing the rights-controlled model by offering a huge selection of images to buyers at significantly reduced prices.

It helps to understand the difference between royalty-free and rights-managed stock. Royalty-free does not actually mean "free," but it gives buyer's permission to use the image in any number of ways, multiple times, for as long as they want—for a one-time fee. There's usually a limit on how many times the image can be reproduced by a client, so publications with a large readership would not choose a standard royalty-free option. The biggest downside is that the buyer does not own the royalty-free image and anyone—including competitors—can use it for the same fee, at the same time, for the same purposes. This faux pas has caused several companies a bit of embarrassment, including Dell and Gateway who featured stock photos with the same model in their 2004 back-to-school campaigns.

Images that are licensed or "rights-managed" charge a fee each time an image is used. The buyer can have exclusive use for a limited time, allowing the photographer or agency to sell the image again when the embargo period is up. Fees are negotiable and are based on factors such as exclusivity, distribution (readership), how long it will be used, and where it will be used (region or country).

Although some photographers receive assignments for stock photos, it's more common for a photographer to take the images on his or her own and submit them later. Working with a stock agency can be a lot of work. You're hustling to provide hundreds of pictures of which the agency may only want a handful of copies. You're also hidden behind a veil of anonymity called the "agency" and the buyers don't know who you, the photographer, are.

How Profitable Is Stock Photography?

The profitability margin for stock photography varies widely. Images can sell for as little as $50 or as much as $2,500, depending on the client and how the image will be used. A photographer can send in 100 images in the hopes the stock agency will choose at least a dozen or more. Depending on the contractual arrangements, the photographer can be paid per image or per usage of that image.

The explosion of internet microstock agencies and improved digital technology has created an environment with easily accessible stock photos provided by professionals, amateurs, and hobbyists, thereby diluting the stock pool and lowering fees considerably. But again, it comes down to how the images are going to be used.

The low budget, dollar-a-pop stock images offered through microstock agencies are primarily being used for small circulation publications like newsletters and in-house presentations or on web pages. But photos that are going to have a large audience need to have a higher level of exclusivity. For example, if a client wants a picture of a child at a birthday party for a PowerPoint® presentation, he or she is not going to care who else uses it. However, if the client wants the picture for a widely publicized advertisement, brochure, or mailer, having exclusive use of the image for a specified time will be important. This is where the photographers who produce special work will shine.

It's important to understand that stock photographers are not phasing out; they are simply reconstructing and streamlining their specialty areas. The quality stock agencies that supply

Beware!

The photographer must be committed to work on schedule, otherwise the client will have the right to terminate the contact and look for a more reliable photographer. Naturally, there may be unavoidable delays due to illness, power outages, or other unforeseen circumstances; there should be language addressing those conditions in the contract.

Tips for Stock Photographers

As discussed in earlier chapters, it's important to find a niche in which to specialize. You want to become well known for that imagery. You also want to avoid shooting subjects that are too generic or saturated in the market (e.g., sports, business). Here are some other tips that may be useful:

- Use digital technology for faster and easier manipulation of images. Breathe new life into old images by scanning and editing them with software like Photoshop®. This saves time and is less costly than reshooting.

- Work with an agency that allows you to interact with the client. Often when this happens and a buyer is looking for a specific picture, the project turns into an assignment.

- Work with an agency that does not require you to sign over exclusivity, giving them sole rights to the image. Avoid work-for-hire arrangements.

- Stock images need to be carefully organized on a disk in categories with detailed descriptions and keywords. Even if the original images are on film, have them scanned for easier viewing and handling. Looking at pictures on the computer screen is much easier than lugging around a light box for transparencies. A better solution may be to upload your images to an online database for easier accessibility.

- Many photographers provide their own stock images on their web sites, circumventing agencies and percentage fees. Using thumbnails on your web site makes it easy for potential customers to browse around and look at their leisure. Just remember to protect your images by scanning at low resolutions or watermarking—or both. (There's more information on how to protect your images in Chapter 13).

images for commercial clients (where the real money is) are very specific and selective about the photographers and material they want.

Working on Assignment

Assignment photography is when a photographer is commissioned to do a specific project by a client—advertising, weddings, portraiture, or any other event. Initially, assignment work was the only type of photography done in the industry, and it's still the most predominant and favored way of doing business today.

Unlike stock photography, which is shot in anticipation of being sold, work does not commence on the assignment until a contract has been negotiated and the photographer is in receipt of the first advance fee. In addition to fees, the photographer working on assignment should also expect to be reimbursed for expenses.

Under terms of the contract, specifications and deadlines are worked out. Some of the issues that should be addressed are: the overall description of the project, date of completion, black and white or color, how many images to be delivered, how will the images be used, and what form: positive, negative, digital.

The licensing terms will also need to be reviewed and negotiated. Most photographers prefer to sell limited rights, maintaining some control and ownership of the images. Of course, the more exclusive the rights, the higher the fee. We will discuss usage fees in more detail in Chapter 12.

If a client buys all rights or this is a work-for-hire, the client will own and be able to use the images in any conceivable way, preventing competitors from having the same or similar images. Both prohibit the photographer from using those images again. An alternative to granting exclusivity to the client is to offer limited rights, insuring the image will not be made available for use in certain markets without the consent of the client. This approach still allows the photographer to resell the image in a noncompetitive market.

4

The Digital Revolution

The introduction of digital photography has created quite an upheaval, with battle lines drawn between film and digital. Traditionalists maintain that film produces sharper photos and digital images are flat and lifeless. Digital enthusiasts enjoy the convenience and technology of their smaller cameras, compared to the bulkier, noisier analog models. Film buffs assert that digital is the lazy man's choice because they don't put as much time and effort into capturing the best shot, while digital users say, "Duh, that's why we use Photoshop®."

Digital vs. Film

Is digital better than film? Are traditional film cameras on their way to becoming rusty relics? They are according to Kodak, Nikon, and Canon, who have all announced their intention to concentrate their sales on digital cameras and equipment.

The reality is both are fine. Sure, film provides more detail than digital; but digital is easier to manipulate. Because digital users don't usually spend as much time trying to figure out the best shot before each click, people mistakenly think digital is faster. Not true. Photographers spend an inordinate amount of time checking their LCD screens, monitoring rapidly draining batteries, changing light sensors, downloading images, and transferring files—not to mention the editing process. Besides, faster does not mean better; it just means faster.

Actually the processing stage is probably the biggest difference between the two art forms. Film prints come to life in the darkroom through careful and precise development. Digital images are electronically enhanced and edited on the computer in the blink of an eye—or click of a mouse. The good news is that you can enjoy the best of both worlds by scanning prints, slides, and negatives, and then using Photoshop® or similar software to edit.

We checked in with our featured photographers and found that Photoshop® was the most popular choice of imaging software. Ray Strawbridge asserts, "There are a lot of things you can do to clean up an image that you never worried about when shooting transparencies. Now you have the flexibility to remove an unwanted lamp cord or correct any image distortions."

In addition to Photoshop,® Michael Weschler also uses the Bridge® software quite a bit, and Carmen Davis finds the less expensive version of Photoshop Elements® suits her digital needs. "It's amazing what you can do with

Stat Fact

By 2010, 90 percent of all professional photographs will be taken with digital cameras, and fewer than 40 percent of pros will use film for any of their assignments, a study by InfoTrends projected. The study, released in 2006 by the Massachusetts-based research firm, found that 70 percent of professional photos taken at that time came from digital cameras, while 65 percent of professionals were still using film for some shoots.

that software," says Davis. "I have taken some of my images and made 20 by 24-inch posters out of them, complete with borders and graphics."

Digital photography has transformed the traditional darkroom into a computer lab. But just because you're not working in a darkroom doesn't make processing digital images easier. In fact, the opposite is true. There are still just as many decisions to make to reach the final outcome. The camera, computer, and software are all tools for creating and developing an image. Playing the keyboard is like playing a piano—some folks do it well; others don't.

In the end, it comes down to personal preference—yours or the client's. "I prefer working with my Canon because the spontaneity of the camera is very quick to use and I don't miss the moment," says Weschler. "However, a client will occasionally request that I use my film camera for magazine covers. There are some publications that still love film and I work with that."

Ira Gostin also uses both film and digital based on the assignment specifications. "I do what's best for the client," he says. "I don't think it's a decision that I should be making." And when he does shoot transparencies, he still scans the images. "You may shoot it on film, but you're going to deliver it digitally."

Film and digital each have their own advantages and disadvantages. Whatever medium you use should start with your creative vision—followed by the right tools—to help you achieve the best results.

Here to Stay

Although it will be many years (if ever) before digital cameras completely replace their traditional counterparts, there are many reasons that professional photographers have added them to their arsenal of equipment. "In terms of smart business, you have to stay abreast with new technology," advises Weschler. "Whether you like it or not—it's here."

After a lot of research, Strawbridge decided to bite the bullet and now shoots strictly digital. "I haven't shot anything on film in over two years," he says. "Once I became involved with the digital revolution, I found that it continued to evolve and I've gone through three to four different generations of digital cameras."

Strawbridge allows that film has it own characteristics and traditional photography is great for fine art. "But in the commercial world, people want things fast, they want it now, and they don't want to wait," he claims. "Digital is just a natural outgrowth of commercial demands." Digital also works best for photojournalists like Gostin because of the convenience and ability to deliver images to publishers with greater speed.

It's true that digital imaging is rapidly replacing traditional photography. Sales for digital cameras and equipment are projected to increase 25 percent annually, while the analog film market steadily declines. However, there will be a need for film photography for many years to come.

Due to easy manipulation, digital imaging has raised some ethical concerns. The old adage, "the camera doesn't lie," doesn't necessarily apply any longer, and many courts will not accept pictures produced by the new technology as evidence.

Many professionals believe that digital images are not as vivid as ones taken with film, especially when printed in larger sizes. This is the reason that some magazine publications still ask for film negatives, particularly for their glossy cover pages. And with traditional photography, you don't have to fret about a dirty sensor messing up every shot. You get a fresh start with each roll of film. There are also many traditional photographers who enjoy the intricacies of working with film and using different techniques. Fine art photographer Jerry Clement, who uses Ilfochrome processing, is one.

Although advancements in digital cameras and reductions in costs are making the new technology part of the mainstream marketplace, many experts urge career photographers to start with traditional film. Weschler agrees. "Even if you are entirely in a digital environment, it makes a stronger quality image if you can bring a sensibility from a traditional environment," he states. "The line is really blurred now, but you have to think intuition and aesthetic first and then think about technique. If you get too technical, it will just fall flat."

Going back to his traditional roots, Weschler says that before he was ready to make the leap into the digital world he wanted to make sure there would be continuity with his work. "I needed to feel comfortable that my portfolio could have a digital image next to one that was shot with negative film, next to another that was shot with slide film. Once I reached that point, I was convinced this new technology was a very useful tool for me to have."

Technology is Not Evil

It may be scary and intimidating, but technology is not evil—unless it falls into the hands of a heretical, lizard-like, Darth Vader wannabe and then we're all screwed. Technology is what gave us cell phones, laptop computers, and TiVo. Technology lets us pay our bills online, send dirty jokes through anonymous emails, and check on the kids via webcam. Technology allows you to cheat and use auto-focus (fess up—everybody does it). Technology is actually pretty cool.

While technology may seem magical, it isn't. It still has to be controlled and manipulated by human hands and minds (at least until the Darth Vader wannabe takes over). Technology comes in the form of neat gizmos and tools designed to make our lives easier—such as a tricked-out digital camera. Digital images are captured the instant a soundless button is pushed, immediately ready for downloading and transmission to a frantic editor or excited grandma.

Just because a digital camera is easier to handle and editing software is relatively uncomplicated, don't become complacent or underestimate photographic skills. The basics of photography still apply, including knowledge of lighting, set arrangements, and creative vision. In other words, you still have to have talent.

Just to show you how much easier things are now, way back in the old days—roughly 15–20 years ago—before all of this cool technology was introduced to the masses, photographers spent a lot of preproduction time on the set. Polaroids were snapped to be scrutinized for lighting, exposure, and composition; transparencies that took hours to process were taken in advance of commercial shoots so adjustments could be made. But with digital imaging technology, photographs are instantaneously available for viewing and purchase or transmission. An example would be portrait photographers who often provide an electronic slide show immediately following a sitting. Or Carmen Davis, who takes her laptop with her to dog show events so that she can download and look at her images before continuing. "People will huddle around my computer and start picking out pictures before I'm done," she says. "Impulse buying is a good thing for business."

Digital photographers say that aside from instant gratification, one of the best features of digital technology is how easy it is to catalog and store their images, while saving a ton of money on film and the cost to process it. But there is always a flip side; in this case, it's the cost of digital equipment, which can sometimes be prohibitive.

Stat Fact

InfoTrends Inc., a market research and strategic consulting firm for the digital imaging and document solutions industry, predicts that U.S. consumer digital camera penetration will account for 81 percent of the market and about 21 million units shipped in 2010.

Photo labs have also felt the impact of the digital revolution and except for a few holdouts (who now have a special niche), most have converted—or at least made room for the new and improved technology. Unfortunately, some photo labs did not survive the transition from film to digital and had to close their doors permanently. Others, who are barely subsisting,

▲

may hold an individual's film for several days until they have enough orders to warrant turning on their equipment.

You've undoubtedly heard the old catchphrase, "Go digital or die!" ad nauseam, but the reality is going digital is not a rags to riches story. If you are a film photographer whose business lacks luster, a brand-new Canon EOS-1Ds Mark II is not going to swing the pendulum back in your favor. You'll have to work that magic yourself.

Focusing on
the Right Path

The first step in starting a new business is to develop a well-thought-out business plan. This is your blueprint for success, which will evolve and change over time as your business grows. Writing your ideas and plans down compels you to think about all aspects of the business and helps you stay focused.

Some entrepreneurs would rather walk barefoot over broken glass than sit down and write a business plan. Other would-be business owners get so caught up in planning every detail that they never get their business off the ground. You need to find a happy medium between these two extremes.

This chapter focuses on a few issues particular to planning a photography business, but they are by no means all you need to consider when writing your plan.

Be a Fan of the Plan

If you're excited about your business, creating a business plan should be an exciting process, not a painful one. It will help you define and evaluate the overall feasibility of your concept, clarify your goals, and determine what you'll need for start-up and long-term operations. Think of it as looking into a crystal ball for an objective and realistic look into the future.

This is a living, breathing document that will provide you with a road map for your company. You'll use it as a guide, referring to it regularly as you work through the start-up process and then during the operation of your business. And if you need to seek outside financing, either in the form of loans or investors, your business plan will be the tool that convinces funding sources that you are worth every penny.

Putting together a business plan is not a linear process, although the final product may look that way. As you work through it, you'll likely find yourself jumping from defining your service package to cash flow forecasts to staffing, then back to cash flow, on to marketing, and back to your service package. Take your time developing your plan. You're making a serious commitment, and you shouldn't try to rush through it in a weekend.

Beware!
When you make a change to one part of your business plan, be sure you think through how that change will affect the rest of your operation. For example, if you start out working exclusively in a studio doing only portraitures, but later decide to go out on location to shoot weddings and other events, will you have to change your equipment needs (in particular, your vehicle)?

Are You on a Mission?

A mission statement is part of your business plan and is actually the heart of your business. It's important to have a clear understanding of the mission of your company, what you are doing, how and where it's being done, and who your clientele is. Problems can arise, however, when that mission is not clearly articulated into a statement, written down, and communicated to others.

Even if you have already started your photography business, there is no time like the present to write out your mission statement. This helps everyone involved see the big picture and keeps them focused on the true goals of the business. At a minimum, your mission statement should define who your primary customers are; identify the products and services you produce; and describe the geographical location in which you operate. For example, your mission statement might read "Our mission is to provide top quality commercial photography at a fair and reasonable price in the Raleigh/Durham area, while assuring that our clients will receive the highest level of attention, commitment, and professionalism."

A mission statement should be short—usually just one sentence and certainly no more than two. A good idea is to cap it at 100 words. Anything longer than that isn't a mission statement and may be confusing and hard to memorize. Your mission statement also doesn't have to be clever or catchy—just accurate. Think of it as a so-called elevator pitch.

Once you've articulated your message, communicate it as often as possible to employees, customers, and suppliers. Print it in advertising brochures and invoices, on employee correspondence, on a wall poster displayed in a prominent place, and post it on your web site.

Time to Write the Plan

Once you've identified the products and services you want to offer and to whom, and have created your mission statement, you're ready to complete your business plan.

Though the specific content of your business plan will be unique, there is a basic format that you should follow. The format ensures that you address all the issues you need to as well as provide lenders and investors with a document organized in a familiar way to evaluate. The main parts of your business plan should include the following:

> **Tip...**
>
> **Smart Tip**
> As an added safekeeping measure, number each copy of your business plan that is distributed. Log the number in a file, along with the name of the person each copy was given to and the date of distribution.

- *Cover Sheet.* The title at the top of the page should identify the document as a Confidential Business Plan. Further down the page add your business name, address, phone number, fax number, e-mail address, and web site. Then list yourself as the owner or proprietor.

- *Table of Contents.* Start building your business plan by using a detailed table of contents as an outline. It will help you to think about the nuts and bolts in planning your business by serving as a guide during the process. Expand the table of contents by adding subsections to the main sections identifying all of the key issues. Don't forget to add relevant page numbers.

Mission Statement Worksheet

To develop an effective mission statement, answer these questions:

1. What products and/or services do we produce or offer?

   _____

   _____

   _____

2. In what geographical location do we operate?

   _____

   _____

   _____

3. Why does our company exist? Whom do we serve? What is our purpose?

   _____

   _____

   _____

4. What are our strengths, weaknesses, opportunities, and threats?

   _____

   _____

   _____

5. Considering the above, along with our expertise and resources, what business should we be in?

   _____

   _____

   _____

6. What is important to us? What do we stand for?

   _____

   _____

   _____

- *Executive Summary.* This section will provide the reader with a brief synopsis of your photography business. Describe the specific business you intend to start and list the reasons you can make it successful. Include your goals, industry analysis, operations, inventory, and start-up timetable. Limit this section to one or two pages by writing approximately one paragraph for each main section of the plan. Consider this your sales page by making the executive summary relevant, interesting, and engaging so that readers will want to continue reading the rest of the plan.

- *Mission Statement.* As discussed earlier, this is an important element of the business plan as it sets the tone and direction this business wants to take in the pages ahead. This section can also be expanded to include statements about your company's vision, values, services, and philosophy.

- *Marketing Plan.* Include an overview of the market and a description of your potential clients by conducting a simple analysis. If you are a commercial photographer, flip through the Yellow Pages or business directory to get a general idea of prospective business owners who could use your services. Wedding photographers can look at wedding announcements in the local newspaper for an estimate of how many couples are getting married each week, month, or year.

  Identify your competition with regard to your specialty and explain how you plan to corner that market. For example, if your niche is advertising photography, you should communicate how you plan to secure assignments when microstock agencies are now in such big demand.

  Discuss in detail the advantages and drawbacks of your location, how you will deal with growth, and your strategy to promote your business.

- *Organizational Plan.* In this section, confirm your legal structure—sole proprietorship, partnership, LLC, or corporation. Discuss your staffing needs and how you expect to meet them. Are you going to have employees who are full time, part time, or as needed? Are they family members or will you go through a hiring process? Identify the consultants and advisors who will be assisting you and the certifications, licenses, permits, and other regulatory issues that will affect your operations. Specify scheduled operating hours, including holidays. Provide short-term objectives for the immediate future as well as long-range goals that you intend to make happen in two, three, or five years.

- *Management Plan.* This is where you basically need to prove that you are up to snuff by demonstrating how you are going to manage your business. If you are homebased, chances are this is a one-person team. That's no problem as long as you are capable of wearing several hats at one time. Highlight your skills and experience for this type of operation by falling back on your resume. If you were formerly a paper pusher, that indicates you can take care of administrative tasks, which is an important part of any business. However, readers are not going to care about your summer stint as a lifeguard—unless you held a supervisory position signifying your ability to handle responsibility and manage people. If you have prior experience as a photographer—even as an amateur—be sure to list that, along with any awards or other special acknowledgments you have received.

No one likes to admit their shortcomings, but this also is the place where you should identify any weaknesses and describe how you plan to overcome them. For instance, if you are a digital stock photographer but have limited knowledge of imaging software, plan to take an online course or sign up for a class at a local community college.

- *Financial Plan.* This is where you show the source(s) of your start-up capital and how you're going to use the money. Include information on real estate, fixtures, equipment, and insurance. You'll also include your financial statements: balance sheet, profit-and-loss statement, break-even analysis, personal financial statements, and personal federal income tax returns.

  Next, take your financial data and project it out for the upcoming year on a monthly basis to show what your business will do. Include a projected income statement for the second year with quarterly estimates, and annual projections for three, four, and five years. Follow the same formula for cash flow statements, along with worst-case income and cash flow statements to show what you'll do if your plan doesn't work.

- *Summary.* Bring your plan together in this section. If you're trying to appeal to a funding source, use this section to reiterate the merits of your plan.

- *Appendices.* Use this for supporting documents, such as your resume, personal and business references, and credit references. Attach a list of where your photographs have been published or exhibited, studio design and layout, marketing studies, sample advertising, copies of leases, and licensing information.

When you think your business plan is complete, look at it with a fresh eye. Is it a true and honest representation of the facts? Is it realistic? Does it consider all the possible variables that could affect your operation? After you're satisfied, show the plan to two or three professional associates whose input you value and trust. Ask them to be brutally honest with their evaluation; you need to know if there are any glaring problems with your plan so you can correct them before they cost you time and money.

Ira Gostin knew that he needed help putting together his business plan, so he enlisted the aid of a counselor provided by the Small Business Development Center (a branch of the Small Business Administration). "I knew the finance side was definitely my weak area and I needed help getting through that," he says. "This is actually a free service, and they helped me put together a business plan with projections so that I could get financing. It's probably the number one resource that I would recommend to other photographers going into business." For more information on where to find an office close to you, go to www.sba.gov.

Know Your Craft

It's assumed that if you are considering starting a photography business that you have some photographic skills, as well as familiarity with basic photography equipment. You may even be a graduate of an accredited school with a degree in photojournalism or fine art. Even so, continuing your education in the photography industry is essential if you want to succeed and stay ahead of the competition. There are many ways to build up those brain cells, whether you want to take a basic college-level photography course or a class on how to use Photoshop.® Here are some ways you can improve your craft.

Back to School

Across America, you will find a number of accredited photography schools that offer training, certificates, and diplomas in photography and digital imaging. These schools enable students to get the necessary credentials to help launch a successful photography career. At the very least, they boost an individual's confidence as she or he acquires more knowledge in the field.

As an adjunct professor of photojournalism at the University of Nevada, Ira Gostin is a firm believer in the power of knowledge. He's now back in school to get his master's degree in marketing. "I still do a little teaching and lecturing on ethics and business," he says. "And once I finish with grad school, I will start doing my national touring seminars again."

Many universities and colleges offer photography courses through their liberal and fine arts programs. You can find schools and courses that meet your requirements by

Where's the Money?

Because of the internet, outside scholarships have become increasingly easy to find. Here are a few sites that you can look into:

Broke Scholar (www.brokescholar.com). More than 650,000 scholarship award listings.

Careers and Colleges (www.careersandcolleges.com). Find scholarships, grants and loans.

Coca-Cola Scholars Foundation (www.coca-colascholars.org). Available to applicants of four-year colleges as well as technical schools and community college programs.

College Scholarships (www.college-scholarships.com). Scholarships, colleges and online degrees.

FastWeb (www.fastweb.com). Scholarships, financial aid and colleges.

FinAid (www.finaid.com). The smart student's guide to financial aid.

Scholarships.com (www.scholarships.com). Find money for college.

Super College (www.supercollege.com). Look for loans and awards for high school, college, grad, and adult students.

When you are applying for scholarships, grants, and loans, pay particular attention to deadlines. Once you've missed them, you've missed out. The earlier you apply, the better your chances of receiving financial aid.

going to the library or searching on the internet, and you can obtain information on tuition and financial aid at the same time.

Typically, these programs offer a combination of classroom and hands-on experience while helping students prepare their portfolios. They can also assist with internships and job placements in the "real world."

The cost of photography courses varies greatly; however, they will not be easy on the wallet. Financing is available in the form of scholarships, grants, and loans. Some of the schools you apply to may also offer their own need- and merit-based scholarships.

▲

Smart Tip

Tip...

There are a number of other highly regarded photography schools that can be found by looking at online school directories such as ArtSchools.com (www.artschools.com) or World Wide Learn (www.worldwidelearn.com).

Distance Learning

Distance learning is one of the fastest growing learning methods for education. This unconventional learning structure allows students to learn on their own time, in the comfort of their own home, at their own pace, while scheduling time around family commitments or work obligations. It does not require formal classroom attendance, which means that a student does not need to reside on campus or even nearby. A student could live 500 miles away and still get a degree from an accredited college. Usually all course work, examinations, reading, research, and writing assignments are done independently through a telecourse or online study program.

The New York Institute of Photography (www.nyip.com) holds claim to being the oldest and largest photography school in the world. Chuck Delany, NYI dean, says that the school provides distance learning to more than 20,000 active students in the United States and over 50 countries abroad. It offers certification in various areas and year-round enrollment, with a student body comprised mostly of adults in the 30- to 40-year-old age range.

Distance education classes can offer full credit hours equivalent to those offered in a traditional course. Or you can sign up for one-time specialty courses and tutorials that are relevant to your business.

Workshops and Seminars

Informative workshops and seminars are continuously offered throughout the country. These are specialty one-, two-, or five-day courses that focus on a particular area in photography, such as darkroom or lighting techniques, how to become a Photoshop® professional, or composition for nature enthusiasts. Many companies like Canon or Nikon provide workshops like the informative digital photography class Carmen Davis attended. You can even take classes on how to market your photography work or the history of photography. Some of these courses are actual tours that travel to exotic places, while others are conducted at a local hotel or vocational school.

"You want to go to workshops and seminars to learn everything you can about the business of photography," says Michael Weschler. "This is one of the best ways to keep abreast with the way usage and licensing fees are determined, the way marketing works, and how art buyers think."

Webinars are another popular way to attend an online seminar either in real time or by downloading the transcript at a later date. Check the community events section

▲

of your local newspaper, call camera shops in your area, and look on the internet to find out when the next workshop or seminar is being offered.

Reading Materials

For your reading enjoyment, your local library or bookstore has a wealth of information on photography, business, marketing, or other relevant areas. Ira Gostin recommends *The Photographer's Guide to Marketing and Self-Promotion* (Allworth Press, 2001) by Maria Piscopo as well as *ASMP Professional Business Practices in Photography* (Allworth Press, 2001). You will find additional publications listed in the Appendix section of this book.

There is also a big selection of specialty photography and business magazines available, such as *Entrepreneur, Photographic Magazine, PC World,* and *Popular Photography and Imaging.*

Become a Photography Assistant

Take a page from Michael Weschler's book of life and consider working as an assistant to other photographers to broaden your experience in the industry. "This can be a pivotal time because you can decide if this really is the career you want to go into," recommends Weschler. "You can also discover the type of photography you may be interested in by learning about different styles, techniques, and specialties." Weschler had initially thought he would have a career in fine art photography until he assisted other photographers and saw the exciting potential of the commercial field.

As an assistant, your primary objective should not be on how much money you can make but on how much knowledge you can gain before stepping out on your own. Initially, you may not have many opportunities to stand behind the camera while on assignment, but learning how to set up props and lighting can be very beneficial. There is real value in working with different photographers so that you can learn a variety of skills and techniques. It also gives you the opportunity to observe how other business models work. "On your first day, you might be sweeping the floor, taking out the trash, or washing the dishes, but you're going to absorb something," says Weschler. "And the great thing is you're getting paid to learn."

Weschler also says there wasn't a lot of fancy equipment in his school. "It wasn't until I was working on professional sets that I discovered all kinds of expensive toys to play with and learn from," he says. "I also learned a lot about the technical side, including different qualities of lighting, understanding what a color meter was and degrees Kelvin."

Just as you would with any employer, do your homework and research the photographers you are considering working with. This will help you to assess their needs and

Smart Tip

Tip...

On the American Society of Media Photographers web site (www.asmp.org), executive director Eugene Mopsik says that working as a photographer's assistant "is a great way to break into the business, so seek out professional photographers in your area." He advises attending meetings sponsored by local and regional professional photography organizations where you can meet and network with other professionals.

be sure they are ethical, trustworthy individuals who will not take advantage of you. And be honest with the photographer with whom you are interviewing. If you do not possess a certain skill set—say so. They need to know what you're bringing to the table. Most photographers will not mind teaching you the ropes if they know up front what your limitations are.

Attend photography events such as local Advertising Photographers of America (APA) or American Society of Media Photographers (ASMP) meetings so that you can introduce yourself to photographers who might be interested in your services. Not only will you learn new information about the industry, you can also meet and network with other photography assistants. Weschler now uses assistants in his business and says that referrals are very helpful. His studio also uses APA sometimes as a resource when looking for a new assistant.

Once you have a list of photographers you would like to contact, approach them in a professional manner by sending them your resume first. This can be done by mail, fax, or e-mail. After a short period, you can then contact them by phone and talk about how you could assist them. Making cold calls is the hard part. You will probably make quite a few of them, but don't give up! Keep in mind that it's all about timing. If you contact a photographer who doesn't need you today, he might in a few months, so maintain visibility and stay on his radar. "Be persistent and don't get frustrated if a photographer isn't calling back," advises Weschler. "They often have a list of people they work with, but eventually, you will get in to meet with them."

Weschler also says that the process of getting work as an assistant is almost identical to the process you will go through as a photographer. "You have to network with other people and learn how to nurture your clients. Someone once told me it's really hard to get new clients—but it's even harder to keep them."

6

Shoot For Accessibility:
Choosing Your Location

One of the main attractions of starting a photography business is that you can start small. But whether you operate from the comfort of your own home or run your business from a commercial location, you need a place to store your equipment, you need to track your progress and inventory, and you'll need the right supplies to set up shop.

The ideal location for your photography business depends on the type of services you are going to provide, how much equipment and cash you have to start with, and what your specific goals are. Basically, your two choices are homebased or a commercial location. If you opt for the latter, you'll have some additional choices to make that we'll discuss in this chapter.

Many photographers start as a homebased operation with no desire to change that status, which offers convenience and flexibility. Others start at home only to be later faced with the need to expand their operation into bigger quarters. Still others set up their studio in a commercial location at the onset, or plan to do so as soon as they have sufficient revenue.

With adequate planning, a photography business can be operated from any type of abode. To decide where to locate, think about what you must have to operate your business, what you'd like to have, what you absolutely won't tolerate, and how much you're able to pay. Give this process the time it needs and deserves by putting these needs and desires down on paper. A poor location choice can be an expensive mistake that is difficult to remedy.

Home Sweet Studio

One of the key benefits of a homebased business is that it significantly reduces the amount of start-up and initial operating capital you'll need. But there's more to consider than simply the up-front cash. You need to be conveniently located so your clients can find you if necessary and so you can get to them—or to other places you need to go— without spending an excessive amount of time traveling.

If your location works, consider your home from a capacity perspective. Do you have a separate room available for your business, or will you have to do paperwork on a corner of the dining room table? You will find it helpful to separate your work area from the rest of the house so you can have privacy when you're working and get away from "the office" when you're not. Can you set up a functional darkroom with all the tools and equipment you'll need? Do you have adequate storage for equipment and supplies? Many photographers who work from home say that having enough storage space is one of their biggest challenges.

The ideal situation would be to set aside a room (or rooms) exclusively for business use. If you can't, do the best you can with the resources and space you have. Remember that to take the home office deduction on your taxes, the IRS requires that you have a room that is used solely for business. If you're only using part of a room, or if your office doubles as a den or guest room, a home office deduction probably wouldn't survive an IRS audit. You can, of course, deduct all other allowable business expenses.

So, what can you deduct in a homebased business? Directly related expenses, which are those that benefit only the business part of your home, and a portion of

> ## Smart Tip
>
> Even though you're homebased, take care that you present yourself as a serious businessperson. If clients visit your home, your office should reflect your professionalism. Also, any other areas of your home that clients may see should be neat, orderly, and create a positive impression.

indirect expenses, which are the costs involved in keeping up and running your entire home. For example, your office furniture and photography equipment are fully deductible as directly related expenses. In the area of indirect expenses, you may deduct a portion of your household utilities and services (electric, gas, water, sewage, trash collection, etc.) based on the percentage of space you use for business purposes. Other examples of indirect expenses include real estate taxes, deductible mortgage interest, casualty losses, rent, insurance, repairs, security systems, and depreciation. You can also deduct other expenses—inventory, storage, supplies, automobile, marketing, etc.—that are legitimate costs of doing business.

Jerry Clement set up his traditional darkroom in the upstairs guest bathroom. "I have everything arranged so that it can be dismantled in fairly short notice," he says. "It's fully functional, and I can develop traditional black and white prints, along with negative color processing."

If converting a den or spare bedroom into an office and work area is not possible, or if your operation requires a large amount of space, you may want to consider transforming the basement or garage into a suitable work area. Ray Strawbridge has the good fortune to have 1,000 square feet area in his basement to use for his photography business. "It has everything including an office, bathroom, and studio," he says. "There used to be a darkroom, but that has since been turned into a computer lab."

Before you invest too much time in planning or setting up a homebased operation, check your local zoning codes and any deed restrictions that may be attached to the property. Many municipalities have ordinances that limit the nature and volume of commercial activities that can occur in residential areas. Find out what, if any, ordinances are in place regarding homebased businesses before applying for your business license.

Choosing a Commercial Location

If you do not have adequate space at home or if you are unable to set up your business because of zoning or other restrictions, you will need to buy or lease space. Studios can be in almost any type of neighborhood or building, including industrial areas, which generally cost less than commercial or retail space.

Starting in a commercial location requires more initial cash than starting from home, but the business you attract can offset the expense. When looking at commercial

▲

Bright Idea

You can often find studios to rent or lease in larger, metropolitan cities that come fully loaded with backgrounds, lights, and sometimes even assistants.

locations, your choice should be guided largely by the specific services you want to provide and the market you want to reach. Keep in mind that buying or renting a facility that can be converted to accommodate your needs will usually be much more economical than building from the ground up.

Before investing in a commercial facility, be sure the surrounding market is favorable for the studio you envision and the location is consistent with your style and image. Will your clients be comfortable coming there? Is the facility accessible to people with disabilities? If you're on a busy street, how easy is it for cars to get in and out of the parking lot?

If you're in a multi-tenant building, find out about the days and hours of service and access. Are the heating and cooling systems left on or turned off at night and on weekends? This could be a problem if you are storing environmentally sensitive chemicals. If you don't have your own entrance, are there periods when the exterior doors are locked and if so, can you have keys?

Commercial Leases

If this is your first venture into the land of leasing, you may find yourself a bit overwhelmed in the beginning. The documents are cumbersome, wordy, and downright hard to understand. And to make matters worse, they are usually written to the landlord's benefit. But take heart; they are also negotiable.

First, you need to understand what the lease documents say. If you are having trouble deciphering the lingo, talk to your realtor or hire an attorney. Second, you need to know exactly what you want out of this transaction before going to the table. A long, drawn-out negotiation process could kill a deal. And third, you need to be reasonable with your demands. You will be surprised at what you can get if you ask nicely. Besides, the initial lease is just the starting point. Lease items that are subject to negotiation are:

- Start of rent and lease amount (include anticipated increases)
- Length of lease
- Termination clause
- Configuration of the physical space
- Tenant improvements
- Tenant's rights and exposures
- Common area maintenance costs

- Construction allowance (use if you need to do a substantial amount of work to get the space ready for occupancy)
- Subleases and assignments (important if you are going to share space or need to get out of the lease early)
- Any other general terms and conditions in the lease.

Before you sign a lease, make sure you have considered everything. How many rent increases have there been during the past three years? How old is the roof? Find out if there are any anticipated repairs coming up in the near future. The more you know, the less risk you will have.

Smart Tip

Tip...

Many cities have large, spacious photography studios available to rent for special assignments. Although his studio is adequate for most jobs, Michael Weschler says he sometimes needs something more deluxe for a bigger production. "There may be a celebrity or advertising shoot where we need a kitchen or more square footage to accommodate the props, so I'll end up renting another studio."

Sharing Space

Not crazy about leasing commercial space, but can't work out of your home? Another option to consider is sharing a studio with one or two other photographers. Naturally, this type of arrangement has its own pros and cons, but the biggest advantage is reducing your rent by at least half. This benefit helps you project the image of a professional operation at a more affordable cost. It's essentially the same as having a roommate, but

What's Your Sign?

Nothing shouts the news that you are open for business louder than an effective, well-done sign. A homebased operation may not be permitted to have a business sign, so check with your local zoning board before having one made. But if you're in a commercial location, you'll definitely want to have a clear, easy-to-see sign so that clients can find you.

Keep in mind that one-inch letters are easily seen 10 feet away, two-inch letters can be seen at 20 feet, and so on. Don't create a sign with letters so small that your clients can't easily read them. And keep the font simple; fancy lettering with flourishes may be difficult to read easily.

Finally, have a professional proofreader check your sign for errors. Don't spend a lot of money just to make a poor impression.

you'll need to work out a written agreement to make sure everyone has a clear understanding of what's expected from each party.

- Decide what days and times each photographer will have use of the studio.
- Will you share an assistant or have your own employees?
- Will you share some of the equipment?
- How will maintenance and cleaning responsibilities be divvied up? (A better alternative may be to outsource those duties.)
- There also needs to be a termination clause in the event one of you splits off before the end of the lease.

Michael Weschler shares a studio in New York City with another photographer. "I shoot mostly on location, so I don't need a full-time studio," he says. "It's a co-op arrangement, so we're not there at the same time. Whatever day or week I'm scheduled for, then the studio is mine to use."

The Pros and Cons of Franchising

Franchising can be a great way to start a new business because even though you are in business for yourself, you're not alone. You can start your new venture with a proven working model, an enthusiastic team of go-getters, and comprehensive hands-on training.

Here's How it Works

In a nutshell, the franchisor lends his trademark or trade name and business model to the franchisee, who pays a royalty and often an initial fee for the right to do business under the franchisor's name and system. The contract binding the two parties is the franchise, but that term is also used to describe the business the franchisee operates.

The best part for the franchisee is the franchisor has already worked the kinks out of the system and is available to help franchisees when new challenges arise. According to the Small Business Administration, most businesses fail from lack of management skills. This is less likely to happen with a franchised business because your franchisor is there to guide you through the maze of business ownership.

Typically, you think of fast food and restaurants when you think of franchising, but virtually every business form has the potential to be

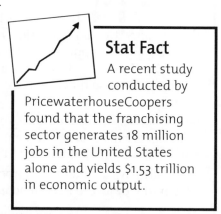

Stat Fact
A recent study conducted by PricewaterhouseCoopers found that the franchising sector generates 18 million jobs in the United States alone and yields $1.53 trillion in economic output.

franchised, and there are a number of franchised photography businesses. In fact, once your business is established, you may want to consider growing it by franchising your concept.

The Cons

While there are many benefits to owning a franchise (security, training, and marketing power), there are some drawbacks. Perhaps the most significant is the cost of a franchise. The initial franchise fee can run anywhere from a few thousand to several hundred thousand dollars. Then, you have continuing royalty payments to the franchisor, based on the weekly or monthly gross income of your business. Additional expenses may include promotional and advertising fees, operating licenses and permits, insurance, and other costs of running a business.

Another big drawback is that you have to give up some of your independence. Each franchise is different in how firm conditions and requirements are; however, you will be bound by the contract to follow and implement the rules and procedures established by the franchisor. For example, if you neglect to pay your royalty fees or misbehave by not meeting performance standards, your franchise could be terminated and you could lose your investment. So, if you like to make your own decisions and "do your own thing," a franchise may not be right for you.

You also have no control over how the franchisor operates, and the corporate office can make decisions that you do not agree with or that reduce your profitability. That's why it's so important to thoroughly research a franchise; you want to see a positive operational pattern before making a commitment.

Much of the information you'll need about a franchise is provided in the form of a document known as the UFOC, or Uniform Franchise Offering Circular. Under Federal Trade Commission (FTC) rules, you must receive this document at least 10 business days before you are asked to sign any contract or pay any money to the franchisor.

Buying an Existing Business

An alternative to a franchise or to starting your own business is to take over an existing studio from a photographer who is retiring or going out of business. Often, this type of business can be purchased lock, stock, and barrel, including photography and office equipment, supplies, backdrops, props, the space itself, and most importantly, a client base. While this may seem like a simple and logical shortcut for anyone starting a new photography business, you should approach this option with caution.

One of the disadvantages of buying a previously owned business is that not only do you get the company's assets, you also assume their liabilities. For example, what

▲

if the building is in serious disrepair or the owner hasn't paid taxes in the last five years? Another concern is losing clientele when the owner leaves. Although the name of business may still be the same, their relationship was with the previous owner, not you. The best-case scenario would be for the owner to hang around for a year or two in an advisory capacity to help everyone feel more comfortable with the transition.

You'll find a variety of businesses for sale advertised in trade publications, local newspapers, on the internet, and through business brokers. But before making a final decision, make sure you have done all of your homework by finding out the following details:

- Find out why the business is for sale. Don't accept what the current owner says at face value; do some research to make an independent confirmation.

- Examine the business's financial records for the previous three years and for the current year-to-date. Compare tax records with the owner's claims of revenue and profits.

- Spend a few days observing the operation. For example, if you're looking at wedding photography business, tag along to a couple of the events.

- What existing equipment and supplies will be transferred to the new owner? What is their condition and will they suit your needs?

- Determine the cost of remodeling if the studio's current setup is not conducive to your future plans.

- Speak with current clients. Are they satisfied with the service? Are they willing to give a new owner a chance? Ask for their input, both positive and negative, and ask what you can do to improve the operation. Remember, even though sales volume and cash flow may be a primary reason for buying an existing business, customers are under no obligation to stay with you when you take over.

- What are the leasing arrangements with the landlord? If there is a mortgage, can it be assumed?

- Consider hiring someone skilled in business acquisitions to assist you in negotiating the sale price and terms of the deal.

- Finally, remember that you can walk away from the deal at any point in the negotiation process before a contract is signed.

Smart Tip

Tip...

If you buy an existing business, include a non-compete clause in your terms of sale. Your new business won't be worth much if the seller opens a competing operation down the street a few weeks after you take over the old company.

7

Business Structure:
A Blueprint for Success

There's a lot to do when you start a business. This chapter addresses some important issues and helps you map out a blueprint for success as you get set up.

A Name to Remember

One of your best marketing tools is the name of your business. A well-chosen name—whether it's your own or a fictitious one—can work very hard for you; an ineffective name means you have to work much harder at marketing your company.

Many photographers use their own name for their business, which has several benefits. One is you don't have to trademark your name because it's already yours. Using your own name not only improves your personal credit as your photography business grows, but it will build prestige within the community. It won't take long for people to recognize your name and associate it with your business.

Just for fun let's see what we can do with the name Sandy Beaches. (You would be surprised to know how many people actually have this name). As part of this exercise, let's say that Sandy is a travel photographer. A short list of possible combinations might include:

1. Sandy Beaches Photography

2. Sandy Beaches, Photographer

3. Sandy Beaches, Travel Photographer

4. Beaches Photography

5. Photography by Beaches

6. Sandy Beaches and Associates

7. Sandy's Photo Lab

This list could easily grow by a couple of dozen names, but this gives you an idea of how to get started by changing elements around. With one exception, these names all clearly indicate what type of business this is. However, number 6 is too vague, making it unclear what services are provided.

On the flip side, you don't want to stunt the growth of your business by its namesake. The name, Sandy Beaches, Travel Photography, unquestionably states the nature of this business; however, if Sandy wants to expand her services to include commercial or portrait photography, the name would no longer be effective.

Okay, so what if your name is something that doesn't roll off the tongue very easily, like Euthanasia Pididiot? Or it has an unpleasant connotation like Robin Banks or John Crapper? (Yes, these are names of real people.) Or worse—what if someone else in the industry or area has the same name for his business? Relax. This is part where we crank up those creative juices and have some fun. Actually, the name "Creative Juices" has been used for several businesses. But not to digress, use the Business Name Worksheet on page 54 and follow along as we guide you down the path of inspiration.

Getting Creative

As mentioned earlier, your business name should very clearly identify what you do in a way that will appeal to your target market. If it's too obscure or cryptic, people will have no idea what your business is. Make the name short, catchy, and memorable—but not cute. There's a fine line between clever and cute. Clever is captivating; cute is comical. Comical is unprofessional. Don't be cute. It should also be easy to pronounce and spell. People who can't say your business name may use your services, but they won't be able to tell anyone else about you.

Though naming your company is without a doubt a creative process, it helps to take a systematic approach. Once you've decided on a name, or perhaps two or three possibilities, check to see if any other business has a similar name. Two different companies with names like Sandy Beaches Travel Destinations and Sandy Beaches, Travel Photographer would probably confuse the public.

Make It Legal

Next, check the name for legal availability. Of course, how you do this depends on what legal structure you choose for your business, which we discuss in the next section. In the meantime, call your local business licensing agency to get more information on registering a fictitious name. If you are a sole proprietor or corporation using the name of the owner(s), you probably will not be required to register it; however, you may still want to consider it so no one else can use that name.

Also, check to see if the name conflicts with any name listed on your state's trademark register. Your state's department of commerce can help you or direct you to the correct agency. You should also check with the trademark register maintained by the U.S. Patent and Trademark Office (PTO), which is listed in the Appendix.

Once the name you've chosen passes these tests, you need to protect it by registering it with the appropriate state agency; again, your state's department of commerce can help you. If you anticipate doing business nationally, you should also register the name with the PTO.

Structure It Legally

No doubt you would much rather set up tripods and polish lens converters, but you need to give some thought to your company's legal structure. Your choice can affect your financial liability,

Smart Tip

Tip...

Look on the internet to see if your chosen name is in use. If someone else is already using your company's name as a domain name, consider coming up with something else. Even if you have no intention of developing your own web site, customers could still be confused if they search online for you.

▲

Business Name Worksheet

List three (or more) variations using your own name for your business:

1. _____

2. _____

3. _____

List three business name ideas associated with your specialty or niche as a photographer (i.e., weddings, commercial, fine art):

1. _____

2. _____

3. _____

List three business name ideas associated with your geographical area. You can use the name of your town, county, or state. Or use something that your area is well known for, such as a southwestern region or pristine beaches.

1. _____

2. _____

3. _____

Once you've narrowed it down to one or two choices, take the following steps:

❏   Write it down to see how it looks

❏   Say it loud to hear how it sounds

❏   Check the first initials of each word to make sure the acronym isn't something inappropriate

❏   Run it by family and friends to see if they are as enthusiastic as you are

❏   Look in the Yellow Pages and on the web to see if someone else is using it

❏   Call the county clerk or secretary of state's office to make arrangements for filing it

the amount of taxes you pay, and the degree of control you have over the company. It can also have an impact on your ability to raise money, attract investors, and sell the business.

So, what goes into choosing a legal structure? If you're starting the business by yourself, you'll be the one making all of the decisions. However, if other people are

of asset protection and limiting your finan-
well.

sed entrepreneurs prefer to be classified as
. It's not unusual for a business owner to
a partner or to incorporate as the business
torship is its simplicity. There's not a lot to
ing fees. But the disadvantage of being a sole
wrong (i.e., you are sued or default on a loan),
al assets and kick you to the curb.

ople go into business together, a partnership
ent can come in handy if you want to share a
sts. Just make sure you have a well-written
p works basically like a sole proprietorship,
ofits, expenses, and liabilities of the business.
ogether.

This type of structure has a lot of the same
poration, but it can reduce the partners' or

ion is comprised of shareholders who elect a
, who then hire employees to manage and
irely possible for a corporation to have only
lly function as a sole proprietorship. The
rporation is in the area of asset protection—
ant to put into the business don't stand liable

es better than another? What's important is
decided to incorporate so that his personal
Clement is in the process of rolling his busi-
armen Davis didn't see a need to incorporate,
Motion.

and where you expect to take your company.
opriate for your particular needs.

need an attorney to set it up? No. There are
d kits on the market, and most of the state
agencies that oversee corporations have guidelines you can use. Even so, it's always a

good idea to have a lawyer at least look over your documents before you file them, just to make sure they are complete and will allow you to function as you want.

Finally, remember that your choice of legal structure is not an irreversible decision; although if you're going to make a switch, it's easier to go from the simpler forms to the more sophisticated ones than the other way around. The typical pattern is to start as a sole proprietor and move up to a corporation as the business grows. But if you think you need the asset protection of a corporation from the beginning, that is how you should start out.

Licenses and Permits

Most cities, counties, and/or states require business owners to obtain licenses and permits to comply with local regulations. While you're still in the planning stages, check with your local planning and zoning department or city/county/state business license department to find out what licenses and permits you will need for your photography business, in what order you need to obtain them, and the procedures involved. This process will probably fall under the "least fun things to do" category because you will spend time on hold and getting the runaround, but it will save you a lot of headaches in the end.

You may need one, some, or all of the following:

- *Occupational license or permit.* This is typically required by the city (or county, if you are not within an incorporated city) for just about every business operating within its jurisdiction. License fees are essentially a tax, and the rates vary widely based on the location and type of business. As part of the application process, the licensing bureau will check to make sure there are no zoning restrictions prohibiting you from operating in your location.

- *Fire department permit.* If your business is open to the public or in a commercial location, you may be required to have a permit from the local fire department.

- *Sign permit.* Many cities and suburbs have sign ordinances that restrict the size, location, and sometimes the lighting and type of sign you can use in front of your business. Landlords may also impose their own restrictions. Most residential

> **Beware!**
> Find out what type of licenses and permits are required for your business while you're still in the planning stage. You may find out that you can't legally operate the business you're envisioning, so give yourself time to make adjustments to your strategy before you've spent a lot of time and money trying to move in an impossible direction.

Laying the Foundation

Deciding what type of business structure you need can sometimes be confusing and overwhelming. Think about the following questions as you ponder this important decision:

- How many owners does your business have? If more than one, what are their roles and will they have equal participation?

- Do you want to be the main or only decision maker?

- How concerned are you about asset protection or tax consequences?

- Is cost a factor in determining your business structure? If so, understand you can always change the structure as your business grows.

- How much paperwork can you realistically handle? Some structures involve more administrative work than others.

- Do you want to be a privately held or public company?

- Will employees be allowed to participate and become part owners in the business?

- Do you want your investors to be shareholders in the business? If so, do you still want to maintain control or share those duties?

Revisit these questions at least once a year. As your business grows, its needs will change and so will some of the structural decisions you previously made.

areas forbid signs altogether. Before you get too artistic, check regulations and secure the written approval of your landlord (if applicable) to avoid costly mistakes,

- *State licenses.* Many states require people engaged in certain occupations to hold licenses or occupational permits. This would also include a license for sales and use taxes, which most states require for anyone (including photographers) engaged in the sale of products and services to clients. Check with your state's department of revenue.

- *Federal licenses.* It's rare, but sometimes federal licensing is required. This is really more for a business that is government regulated. However, if you are conducting business across state lines or running ads in another state, contact the Federal Trade Commission. Then consult with an attorney who can guide you through the application process.

Covering Your Assets

In the absence of a crystal ball, you can't possibly foresee each and every hazard lurking around the corner that might potentially jeopardize your livelihood. However, you can take the necessary steps to protect you and your business with adequate insurance. Sit down with an insurance agent who is familiar with your type of business, analyze your potential risks and exposures, and then purchase appropriate and sufficient coverage.

- *Homeowner's insurance.* Chances are your homeowner's or renter's policy will not provide enough coverage for inventory and equipment, so you will need to add a rider to your existing policy.

- *Property insurance.* This type of policy covers the building and contents (including equipment) in the event of damage, theft or loss.

- *Contents insurance.* If you are leasing studio space, contents insurance will reimburse you in the event of destruction, damage or theft.

- *General liability insurance.* This will protect you and your business from liability in the event someone—customer or an employee—sues you for personal injuries or property damage. Let's say your assistant trips over a tungsten light and burns his leg. If he decides to sue you for loss of wages and punitive damages, the cost of defending yourself could be prohibitive. That's why this type of insurance is so important.

- *Umbrella policy.* This basically covers your other insurance policies like property, casualty, and general liability in case they exceed their limits when a claim is filed.

- *Business interruption insurance.* This protects you from loss of revenue in the event of property damage or loss. For example, if you were unable to conduct business because a storm caused extensive damage to your studio, you would be reimbursed for rents, taxes, and income that would have been earned during the down time.

- *Disability and health insurance.* Let's face it, life happens. No matter how young or healthy you are, there is always the possibility you may be thrown a curve ball that could cause a serious setback. There are numerous kinds of health and disability policies that can be customized to fit your lifestyle and budget if you should ever become sick, injured, or disabled.

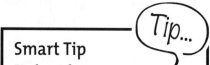

Smart Tip

Find out from your insurance agent what documentation the insurance company requires in the event of a claim—especially for inventory and equipment. This way you will be sure to maintain accurate records and have them available if you need to file a claim report.

- *Life insurance.* Okay, so what if life really zaps you? Will your untimely demise create a financial hardship for loved ones? Tough things to think about, but it really pays to be prepared for the unexpected.

Unfortunately, there is not a one-plan-fits-all insurance policy. But a qualified insurance agent can help you anticipate unforeseen events, evaluate your risks, and determine which ones you need to insure against.

People You Should Know

As a business owner, you may be the boss, but you can't be expected to know everything. There are going to be times and situations when you'll need to turn to other professionals for information and assistance. Now is the time to go ahead and establish relationships with these professionals *before* you get into a crisis situation.

To look for a professional service provider, ask friends and associates for recommendations. You might also check with your local chamber of commerce or trade association for referrals. Find people who understand your industry and specific business and appear eager to work with you. Keep in mind that you are going to have a personal relationship with these people, so it's important that you feel at ease with them. If you hit a snag, they will be the ones who'll help to bail you out. So check them out with the Better Business Bureau and the appropriate state licensing agency before committing yourself. The professional service providers you're likely to need include:

- *Accountant.* Whether directly or indirectly, your accountant will most likely have the greatest impact on the success or failure of your business. A good accountant will always be aware of the ever-changing tax laws and how they apply to your business. He can counsel you on tax issues if you are forming a corporation as well as advise what types of business deductions you are eligible for. Your accountant can assist in charting future actions based on past performance, help you organize statistical data, and advise you on your overall financial strategy with matters related to your business goals. A good accountant will also serve as a tax advisor, making sure you are in compliance with all applicable regulations and that you don't overpay any taxes.

- *Attorney.* Look for a lawyer who practices in the area of business law, has a good reputation, and values your patronage. Interview several attorneys and choose one with whom you feel comfortable. There is usually no charge for an initial consultation, but make sure to clarify this before making an appointment. Good attorneys don't come cheap, so you'll also want to establish the fee schedule ahead of time and get your agreement in writing. Once you have retained an attorney, let him or her review all contracts, leases, letters of intent, and other legal documents before you sign them. He or she can also help you collect bad debts and establish personnel policies and procedures. And whenever you are unsure of the legal ramifications of any situation, call your attorney immediately.

- *Insurance agent.* A good independent insurance agent can assist you with all aspects of your business insurance, from general liability to workers' compensation, and probably even handle your personal lines as well. Look for an agent who works with a wide range of insurers and understands your particular business. There are many different types of coverage. Your agent should be willing to discuss the various details, while helping you determine the most appropriate coverage. He should also help you understand the degree of risk you are taking and what remedies are available to minimize risks. Even more importantly, your agent should assist with expediting any claims that may arise.

- *Banker.* In addition to a business bank account, you should have a good relationship with a banker. The bank you've always done your personal banking with may not necessarily be the best bank for your business. Talk to several bankers before making a decision on where to place your business. Maintain your relationship with your banker by reviewing your accounts periodically and making sure the services you use are the most appropriate ones for your current situation. Ask for advice if you have financial questions or problems. When you need a loan or a bank reference to provide to creditors, the relationship you've established will work in your favor.

- *Other Experts.* As your business grows you may find the need to seek the services of other types of professionals in various, related fields. A business consultant can help you evaluate your business plan; a marketing consultant can assist you with marketing strategies; and a human resources consultant can teach you how to avoid costly mistakes when you are ready to hire employees. There is also the computer expert who can help you maintain, trouble-shoot, and expand your system as needed, while a web designer can develop a professional looking site for your business.

No matter how good you are at what you do, chances are you can't do it all—and you shouldn't—so find ways to network and get in touch with professionals who can help make your business a success. Even the president of the United States admittedly doesn't know everything. That's why he surrounds himself with advisors—experts in particular areas who provide knowledge and information to help him make decisions. Savvy small-business owners use a similar strategy. This frees them up to focus on building and growing their respective companies.

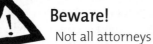

Beware!

Not all attorneys are created equal, and you may need more than one. For example, the lawyer who can best guide you in contract negotiations may not be the most effective counsel when it comes to copyright issues. Ask about areas of expertise and specialization before retaining a lawyer.

8

Business Equipment
for the
Photographer

Many small businesses can be started with equipment their owners already have. Of course, your equipment needs for the photography side of the business will be different than your equipment needs for your office set-up. You don't need every single piece of equipment listed in this chapter to get started, but at least you have some things to consider and decide how they work in relation to your own goals and growth strategy.

Equipping Your Office with the Right Stuff

Most entrepreneurs love trotting down to the local office supply and equipment store. It's easy to get carried away when you're surrounded by an abundance of clever gadgets, so discipline yourself to get only what you need. For starters, consider these basic items:

- *Computer and Printer.* A computer with a color printer is absolutely essential for any business—and especially photography. In addition to editing and producing images, it can help you manage bookkeeping and inventory control tasks, maintain client records, create a web site, and produce marketing materials.

- *Software.* Think of software as your computer's "brains," the instructions that tell your computer how to do what you need it to do. As discussed in Chapter 4, The Digital Revolution, there are many types of programs on the market that edit, enhance, organize, and print images. There are also a number of systems to handle your accounting, inventory, client information management, and other administrative requirements. Software can be a significant investment, so do a careful analysis before making a final decision.

- *Modem.* This goes along with the computer because modems provide essential access to the internet. Invest in the fastest cable modem or DSL that your budget will allow to accommodate the size and volume of images you will be transmitting.

- *Data and Equipment Protection.* In the event of a power failure or brownout, you'll need an uninterruptible power supply to keep your computer from going down, and a surge protector to protect your system from power surges. You'll also need a data backup system that allows you to copy the information

Bright Idea

If your office has a large volume of outgoing mail, consider leasing a postage meter. These instruments allow you to pay for postage in advance and print the exact amount on the mailing piece when it is used. Meters also provide a "big company" professional image, are more convenient than stamps, and can save you money in a number of ways. Your local post office can provide you with more information.

from your computer to another location for safe storage. This is exceedingly important for digital photographers who have hundreds of images stored on their computers.

- *Postage Scale.* A postage scale is a valuable investment for business owners because it takes the guesswork out of calculating postage and will quickly pay for itself.

- *Photocopier.* The photocopier is a fixture of the modern office and can be very useful to even the smallest business. In addition to making copies for clients, it will also be handy for copying invoices, checks, schedules, marketing materials, etc. The larger your operation, the more likely you are to need to make photocopies of a variety of things.

> ## ⚠ Beware!
> Though integrated, multifunction devices such as a copier/printer/fax machine or a fax/telephone/answering machine may cost less to acquire and take up less space in your office, you risk losing all these functions simultaneously if the equipment fails. Also, consider your anticipated volume of use with the machine's efficiency rating and cost to operate and compare that with stand-alone machines before making a final decision.

- *Fax Machine.* As with a photocopier, the larger your operation, the greater the chance that you'll need fax capabilities. Although you can add a fax card to your computer, it must be on to send or receive faxes, and the transmission may interrupt other work. A stand-alone machine with a dedicated phone line may be a better investment.

- *Paper Shredder.* In response to a growing concern for privacy and the need to recycle and conserve space in landfills, shredders are becoming increasingly common in both homes and offices. They allow you to efficiently destroy incoming unsolicited direct mail as well as sensitive internal documents, such as old client files and financial papers, before they are discarded.

- *Shelving.* Most business owners will tell you that having shelves installed on the walls of your office or studio is essential to keeping inventory and supplies organized and within easy reach. You can also purchase storage shelves on wheels or a shelving unit that comes as one large piece of furniture.

Telecommunications

Advancing technology gives you a wide range of telecommunications options. So wide, in fact, that it has become increasingly confusing for consumers to know where to look first. Shopping for phone service now ranks right up there with looking for used cars and life insurance on the list of things to avoid in life. Start by contacting your local telephone service provider and ask to speak with someone who can assess your needs. Most telephone companies have created departments dedicated to small and homebased businesses, and they can help you put together a service and equipment package that will work for you—usually at a discount. Specific elements to keep in mind include:

- *Telephone.* Whether you are homebased or in a commercial location, two telephone lines should be adequate during the start-up period. As you grow and your call volume increases, you can add more lines. Your telephone can be a tremendous productivity tool, and you'll want to consider additional features such as automatic redial, speed dial, call forwarding, call waiting, and a speakerphone for hands-free use. These services are typically available through your telephone company for a monthly fee.

- *Answering machine/voice mail.* Because your business phone should never go unanswered, even after regular business hours, you need a reliable answering device to take calls when you can't do it yourself. Whether to buy an answering machine or use the voice-mail service provided through your telephone company is a choice you must make depending on your personal preferences, work style, and needs.

- *Cellular phone.* Once considered a luxury, cell phones have become standard equipment not only for businesspeople, but also for just about everyone. Most have features similar to your office phone, and equipment and services packages are very reasonably priced. Features such as digital images, text messaging, e-mail, and news services are becoming increasingly available and affordable.

- *Toll-free number.* If you expect to have clients outside your local calling area, you may want to consider providing them with a toll-free number so they can reach you without having to make a long-distance call. Most long-distance service providers offer toll-free numbers and have a wide range of service and price packages. Shop around to find the best deal for you.

- *E-mail.* E-mail allows for fast, efficient, 24-hour communication and is an essential tool for any business. Check your messages regularly and reply to them promptly.

The Photographer's Case

What kind of photography equipment do you need to succeed? Truthfully, there are too many variables to provide you with clear-cut suggestions. Your needs will largely be dependent on what type of photography you do (digital or traditional) and your budget.

Jerry Clement's traditional homebased darkroom features the basic enlarger, a couple of easels, color analyzer with a timer and a grain focuser, along with a heated and

Lights, Camera, Click

When designing a studio, part of the process includes deciding what type of base lighting to install. Floor-based lighting is when you have light stands and background supports that are designed to be lightweight and easily portable. Of course, you will need to watch your step so as not to stumble over the lighting equipment.

A ceiling-based studio has mounted background rollers and a rail system for flexible positioning. It also frees up floor space for your other equipment and furnishings. This is generally the preferred method, although it typically costs approximately $1,000 more than floor-based lighting.

The basic types of lighting are:

- **Main light.** Primary source of illumination.
- **Fill light.** Lightens shadows created by other lighting.
- **Background light.** Brings up the level of illumination between the subject and the background.

As for how much lighting you will need in terms of watts—that really depends on what format camera is used and how big the subject being photographed is. For example, head and shoulder portraits require much less light than vehicles or other large objects. Also, if your studio has windows, you can utilize natural sunlight.

Matters of Light and Depth (April, 1999) by Ross Lowell is an excellent primer on lighting techniques and equipment to help photographers conquer "lighter's block." Lowell writes, "The problem is that there are so many tools, techniques and terms, so many options and mysteries, that attempting to light even a simple scene can be a paralyzing experience." In his book, he helps to break down the mysteries of studio lighting in plain, simple terms about how different types of lighting work they way they do and how to utilize them to your best advantage.

thermostatically controlled processor. "The processor is a basically a vertical tank with four divisions in it," he says. "You can put different chemicals in each slot and it takes up a lot less space than the traditional trays."

It goes without saying that a camera is a basic necessity; however, many professionals believe it is the least important item in your case. They consider the lenses and accessories a higher priority that requires a bigger investment. There are many different kinds of lenses, but the three basic types are normal, wide, and telephoto. Event photographers typically use wide aperture lenses, while macro lenses are used for close-up shots of small objects like flowers or jewelry. Lens filters like UV or polarizing filters should be part of the package. Carmen Davis regularly swaps around three different lenses, but there is another one that she longs for. "I lust for the 500 mm to use for long lure coursing shots," she confesses. "But that is a very expensive lens and I haven't decided if it's worth the investment; I'll probably rent it first."

Filters, strobes, and flashes are also great tools to have, along with light meters, tripods, and a really big bag to carry all this stuff in. The more immersed you become in your field, the more ravenous you'll be for the latest and greatest in photographic gadgets and gizmos, so pace yourself—and stick to your budget.

Keep in mind that it takes a lot more than expensive equipment and a fully stocked studio to be a successful photographer. These are simply tools to make it easier and more convenient for photographers to create the desired images; they are not going to turn a mediocre photographer into a good one. That part is up to you. In *The Complete Idiot's Guide to Portrait Photography* (Alpha, 2002), Kathleen Tracy affirms that by writing, "There hasn't been a camera invented yet that can independently decide when to press the shutter. The art involved is the photographer's inner sense of knowing just when to take the picture."

New vs. Used

When it comes to purchasing new or used equipment, the lines are clearly drawn as photographers take up their positions on each side of the fence. Clement buys most of his equipment used in an effort to keep costs down. "You can find some really good bargains in used equipment if you look, but you have to know what you're looking for," he cautions. He makes regular online purchases—equipment and supplies—from a couple of wholesale houses in New York. Clement has also had good luck buying used equipment on eBay. "However, I don't recommend purchasing supplies like paper, chemicals, or film on eBay, because you can't be sure how fresh it is or if it came from a climate controlled environment or a hot warehouse."

On the other side of the fence, you will find Michael Weschler who doesn't generally like to buy used equipment because it doesn't have a warranty and he doesn't know its quirks. "All cameras and equipment have their own idiosyncrasies and if you buy them used, it just compounds things," he says.

Equipment Rental

Before you get too carried away or feel overwhelmed at the thought of owning equipment that may only get minimal use, know that renting equipment is an option available to photographers. "Every assignment is unique and often requires different equipment and props," advises Weschler. "It doesn't make sense to buy something for $30,000 that you're only going to use a couple of times."

Weschler says the same rules of rental also apply to props; you can rent just about anything. "If you need a helicopter to get a certain shot, you're not going to buy it—you're going to rent it," he says. "Or let's say you're doing a set that requires 100 sandbags and 50 feet of black velvet. You're not going to buy that stuff; you're going to rent it along with the truck to carry it in."

Also, take a tip from Davis, who recommends before you purchase an expensive lens or other piece of equipment, that you rent it and try it out first.

Burglar-Proof Your Business

Whether you are homebased or in a commercial location, you need to be sure that your facility is safe and secure for you, your employees, and your clients. And, of course, you also want to protect your equipment and any inventory you might have. Most people know that photography equipment fetches a pretty high price, so you should take protective measures to prevent theft.

Look into your area's crime history to determine what steps should be taken to safeguard your business. Contact your local police department's community relations department or crime prevention officer to find out if your studio's location has a higher-than-desired crime rate. Most will gladly provide free information on what kind of security measures are needed.

▲

Batten Down the Hatches

Take preventive steps to protect your computer from intruders. Imagine that your computer is a brick and mortar business stocked with cash, sensitive documents, inventory, and expensive equipment. You're not just going to let somebody walk in and clean you out. You're going to protect your business with an alarm, a padlock, and a safe. Well, your computer has to be secured in pretty much the same way. Recommended safety measures include:

- Installing a firewall in your computer

- Updating your virus software on a regular basis and scanning your computer frequently

- Changing your password often, with a different one for each account, and making sure to never, ever give them out to anyone

- Making online transactions using a credit card (not a debit card) or a secure online payment service like PayPal.

Some will even personally visit your site to discuss specific crime prevention strategies. Many also offer training seminars for small businesses and their employees on workplace safety and crime prevention

Thanks to technology and the growing concern for security issues, the cost of electronic surveillance equipment is dropping. Many insurance companies offer discounted premiums when these devices are installed. You can also increase the effectiveness of your security system by discretely posting signs in your windows and around your facility announcing the presence of that equipment.

9

Help Wanted:
Staffing Your
Studio

Many professional photographers are very content running their businesses as solo operators, handling everything from answering e-mails to transporting photography equipment to location shoots and setting everything up. There is certainly nothing wrong with this strategy, but if your plan is to expand your business, there will be a point at which you will need to hire people. And even if your goal isn't growth, there are still times when solo operators need assistance, so it will help if you understand the nitty-gritty details involved in finding, hiring, and managing employees.

If you've never supervised or managed people before, you may find it difficult to turn over tasks to someone else. The best way to get around this obstacle is to just do it. Of course, it helps to have a hiring plan, which we're going to assist you with in this chapter.

Part of that plan is to hire people *before* you desperately need them. If you wait until the last minute, there is a potential for hiring mistakes that can cost you dearly, both in terms of cash and quality of service.

Another component of the staffing plan is to establish a pay scale. Of course, this depends on what you are hiring people to do, the skills needed, and the salary ranges in your area. You can get a good idea of the pay ranges in your area by checking the classified ads in the local paper or talking to other photographers. To find out national average pay scales for a variety of positions, go to the web site for the U.S. Department of Labor, Bureau of Labor Statistics at www.bls.gov.

The Hiring Process

The first step in the hiring process is deciding exactly what you want someone to do. You know you need help, but exactly what kind of help? Do you need someone to monitor the phones and schedule appointments or an assistant to accompany you to location shoots? Initially, you'll look for people to do the tasks you can't or don't want to do. As you grow, you'll be looking for people who can help you expand your capabilities like Michael Weschler, who was a second camera for one of the photographers he assisted years ago.

Next you will need to write out a job description that includes all responsibilities, including the physical requirements of the job such as setting up equipment or handling sensitive chemicals. This forces you to think about the type of person who will best meet your needs, which reduces the risk of hiring the wrong person. Plus, it gives you something to show applicants so they are able to tell if the job you are offering is the one they want.

The job description doesn't have to be long and formal, but it needs to clearly outline the person's duties and responsibilities—perhaps producing finished photos in the studio's darkroom or making sales calls to potential clients. It should also list any special skills or other required credentials like a certificate for digital

Smart Tip

Tip...

Compare salary ranges in your area with those in other parts of the country by using the salary wizard at Salary.com (www.salary.com).

imaging, or a valid driver's license and clean driving record for someone who is going to be driving a vehicle as part of their job. To help sharpen the focus of your thinking lens, use the Job Description Worksheet on page 72

Establish basic personnel policies so that everyone knows who's doing what and when they're supposed to be doing it. Don't think that because you're a small company, you can just deal with personnel issues as they come up. For example, clearly define what fringe benefits you offer and who is eligible to receive them; spell out working hours as well as sick days, holidays, and vacation; explain what conduct is unacceptable on the job and how the disciplinary process works. You'll avoid a lot of problems down the road if you set policies in advance.

You should also ask prospective employees to fill out a job application form—even if it's someone you already know and even if he or she has submitted a detailed resume. A resume is not a signed, sworn statement acknowledging that you can fire them if they lie—an application is. The application also helps you verify a resume, so compare the two and make sure the information is consistent. You can get a basic job application form at most office supply stores or you can create your own. You may also want to have your attorney review the form you will be using for compliance with the most current employment laws.

Building Your Dream Team

One of the biggest challenges for any business is finding and keeping qualified people on staff. Be creative and look for alternatives to the standard help-wanted classified ad. Network among people you know, put notices on bulletin boards in churches and community areas, leave flyers at photography shops, and check with college placement offices. In short, go to the candidates, don't wait for them to come to you.

Flexibility is a key ingredient to finding good people, and there are lots of talented folks who either don't want to work full time or need to work unusual hours. This type of arrangement can be beneficial when you are just starting out and are unsure about your workload. As your business grows and you need to extend the hours or decide a full-time person should do that particular job, you can change the status of that employee. Or, if that doesn't work, consider hiring a second part-timer, setting up a

Job Description Worksheet

Date: _____ **Job Title:** _____

Objective (write brief statement of job's purpose):

_____

_____

Hours per Day/Week/Month: _____

Responsibilities:

Job Duties   Frequency

1. _____   _____

2. _____   _____

3. _____   _____

4. _____   _____

5. _____   _____

Required Skills:

_____

_____

Required Education/Knowledge:

_____

_____

Required Licenses, Certifications, Permits:

_____

_____

Working Conditions:

❑ Seated   ❑ Traveling   ❑ Other:

❑ Stooping   ❑ Driving   _____

❑ Climbing   ❑ Handling/Setting Up   _____
                        Photo Equipment   _____

❑ Reaching   _____

❑ Lifting   ❑ Working with   _____
                        Chemicals

▲

> **Tip...**
>
> **Smart Tip**
>
> Wages are only part of an employee's total compensation. Add more perks to the package by including health insurance, paid holidays, and vacations. An added incentive could be an annual bonus.

job-sharing situation, or some other solution that lets you to retain a valuable person and still get the work done.

A Family Affair

Nepotism is very common among small business owners; however, just because someone is a family member or close friend doesn't mean she or he is the best choice. While keeping it in the family has its merits—loyalty, continuity, and dependability—there is also the danger of someone taking advantage of the working situation. For example, if your nephew is working as a part-time assistant, you might not think twice about assuming he will accompany you at the last minute to a weekend shoot. But what if he's already made other plans and he's resentful because his dad still insists he go with you? And will you look the other way if your sister decides to stroll in an hour or so late every week while she checks out garage sales on her way to work?

These types of situations can often be difficult to address unless there are firm policies and procedures in place. Once those have been established, Sis will know she is expected to monitor the phones and schedule appointments from 10:00 A.M. to 2:00 P.M. on Tuesdays, Thursdays, and Fridays. And your nephew can rest assured that you are not going to mess up his weekend plans unless it is a prearranged event involving plenty of notice.

Independent Contractors

An alternative to going through the process of hiring employees is to use independent contractors. Of course there are advantages and disadvantages, but more importantly, you need to understand the difference so you can avoid unnecessary and costly mistakes at tax time.

As an employer, you will pay payroll taxes, workers' compensation insurance, unemployment benefits, and any other employee benefits you may decide to offer. An independent contractor is self-employed and will pay his or her own taxes and insurance, and file the requisite forms with the IRS.

Of course, you have greater control over employees than you do over independent contractors. Employees must comply with company policies and with instructions and directions they receive from you or a manager. You can set their hours and other conditions of employment, along with their compensation package.

Michael Weschler says that everyone, including his studio manager, is an independent contractor. "For each assignment, I need different people to do different

> **⚠ Beware!**
> Correctly classifying workers is important, and failing to do so can result in severe penalties. The fine for an intentional misclassification can be a penalty equal to 100 percent of the amount of taxes owed.

things," he says. "I can't always fly my regular assistants from New York to wherever I'm going, so I will hire other independently contracted assistants in other cities for that particular job."

If you use independent contractors, you should have a written agreement that describes the services to be performed, the anticipated timeframe in which they are to carry out those duties, and how much they will be paid. The agreement can also be instrumental in confirming that the person is indeed an independent contractor and not a salaried employee in the event the IRS or any other agency questions the working relationship. For more information, consult your accountant or tax advisor, or see Publication 15-A, *Employer's Supplemental Tax Guide*, which is available from the IRS.

Short-Term Solutions

From time to time, your staffing needs may fluctuate. This can be especially true around holidays when you may have a backlog of rush orders. Perhaps a special project requires an additional person for a brief interim. Or a regular full-time staff member becomes ill or takes a vacation, leaving a vacancy for a short period.

Before the situation becomes overwhelming, consider using an employment service as a source for temporary help. Many entrepreneurs feel they can't afford the fee, but with the agency handling the advertising, screening, and background checks, the fee isn't quite so large after all.

You may also find that certain tasks can be handled by an independent contractor or consultant. Consider outsourcing work in the areas of accounting and record-keeping, special marketing projects, etc. If you have tasks you need help with but that don't fit the parameters of a regular part- or full-time position, look for nontraditional ways to get them done.

Workers' Compensation Insurance

In most states, if you have three or more employees, you are required by law to carry workers' compensation insurance. This coverage pays medical expenses and replaces a portion of the employee's wages if he or she is

> **Bright Idea**
> Contact area law firms who specialize in employment law and find if they offer seminars or newsletters to the general public. Most will be happy to add you to their mailing lists at no charge.

Student Aid

Many schools offer internship programs. Contact your local university or community college to find out what the requirements are for hiring an unpaid intern who is interested in learning more about photography.

Part of the process requires you to complete an application describing the position (this is where the job description comes in handy) and what you need in terms of skill level—beginner, intermediate, or advanced. The school will then try to match you with qualified applicants and send you their resumes for consideration. Typically, the internship program will stipulate how many hours the intern can work each week or month, as well as what tasks the student may or may not be allowed to do.

injured on the job. Even if you have only one or two employees, you may want to consider obtaining this coverage to protect both them and you in the event of an accident.

Details and requirements vary by state. Contact your state's insurance office or your own insurance agent for information so you can be sure you're in compliance.

Marketing
Made Easy

Brace yourself for a painful truth: To make it as a professional photographer, your marketing skills will have to be better than your artistic ability. Ouch. And all this time you probably thought a good eye and a fully stocked studio would take you from rags to riches. Not true. How do you think these successful photographers were able to stock their studios and

▲

buy their equipment? They started in the trenches just like you beating the bushes while lugging their camera equipment around.

Most photographers do not enjoy the prospect of marketing but it can actually be a lot of fun as you devise clever and innovative ways to fill the coffers. To do that, we're going to talk about different marketing tips, tricks, and techniques that will encourage clients to take a closer look at your services, while you are identifying the competition and learning how to rise above it.

Whether you're on a tight budget or have a boatload to spend on marketing, you've got lots of options. The most important thing to keep in mind about marketing is this: It's not an expense; it's an investment in your business.

Network, Network, Network!

Word-of-mouth will ultimately be your best and most reliable source for promoting your photography business. Tell everyone about your new venture, including family, friends, co-workers, business associates, neighbors, church members, and members of any civic, professional, or fraternal organizations to which you belong.

Develop relationships with anyone you can think of who comes into regular contact with your target market. For instance, if you are a wedding photographer, get to know bridal shop owners in your area so they will recommend your services. Reciprocate by handing out the shop's business cards or fliers to brides who seek your services.

Join Professional Associations

Join local associations, organizations, and civic clubs, especially those affiliated with photography or any other business communities that you can share information, resources, and services with. For example, Business Networking International (BNI) is a professional networking organization that passed 4.9 million referrals last year through member word-of-mouth recommendations. The American Society of Media Photographers (www.asmp.org) offers educational programs and networking opportunities in more than 39 chapters across the United States. Ray Strawbridge is co-president of his local ASMP chapter and says, "Anybody who is going to do photography as a living would do well to get involved with a professional organization."

Ira Gostin, who has been heavily involved with the ASMP and has written a number of articles for its web site, concurs. "Join an association, go to their seminars, and learn from your peers," he advises.

Find out when your local chamber of commerce, Rotary Club, or Toastmasters group holds meetings that you can attend, and exchange business cards with new

Smart Tip

Tip...

The internet is changing the way people shop for photographers, just as it is changing everything else, according to trade groups such as the Professional Photographers of America. On the PPA site alone (www.ppa.com), 117,000 people used the organization's database to look for a photographer in 2004.

acquaintances. There is a wealth of information you can learn from small-business owners in other industries who have successfully carved out a niche for themselves.

Get on Your Soap Box

Hit the "rubber chicken circuit." Make yourself available as a speaker to every professional, fraternal, and service organization in town. Many of these groups meet weekly, and they are always looking for speakers. You may not get paid, but you'll get a free meal, make some valuable contacts, and get the word out about your business.

Develop a 15- to 20-minute presentation about an aspect of the services you provide that includes a PowerPoint slideshow with some of your best images. Keep the information you provide helpful, but general—don't make this a sales pitch for your business. Have business cards and brochures or some other useful handout to distribute at the end of your presentation.

Some possible topics for your presentation could include mastering the basics of digital photography, artistic interpretation, or tips on shooting animals or nature.

Get a list of all the organizations that might be receptive to having you speak and send a letter introducing yourself and offering your services. Some examples are:

- Kiwanis Club
- Garden clubs
- 4-H clubs
- Nature clubs
- AAA or church events
- Theater groups

The chamber of commerce or public library can provide you with a more comprehensive list of networking opportunities within the community.

If you want to do a more in-depth presentation, consider offering seminars. Seminars help your market learn to use your services more efficiently. They give you the opportunity to show, not tell, what you are all about. If someone is interested enough to attend a free half-day seminar on digital imaging techniques or lighting basics, chances are they'll choose yours. The goodwill that comes from giving your market "something for nothing" is immeasurable and goes a long way toward building client loyalty. Gostin, who taught photojournalism for many years, is a much sought after professional speaker and has delivered workshops across the country about marketing, customer service, and photography.

Advertising and Public Relations

Advertising and public relations are the two key ways you'll promote your business to the public. Where and how you choose to advertise will depend on your budget and your goals.

Direct Mailing

Because of its ability to target well-defined geographical areas, direct mail can be a very effective way to promote your photography services. It also allows you to send a personalized sales message. Several of the photographers interviewed for this business guide, including Michael Weschler, find that direct mail—whether it's a catalog, letter, flier, or coupon—is an efficient way of targeting customers.

There is no magic formula when using direct mail, except that using a solo mailer is more successful than including your information in a cooperative mailer full of supermarket coupons. Depending on what services you offer, you can send a flashy postcard, informative brochure, or sales letter with a personal touch.

Postcards generally get more attention than letters; however, with a sales letter you can also include a response card that encourages a prospective client to contact you for more information. Statistically, a 1 percent direct mail response rate is considered excellent, so if you mail 1,000 pieces and receive 10 phone calls, that is a great turnaround.

Mailing lists can be purchased from list brokers, which you can find in your Yellow Pages under "Advertising—Direct Mail." These lists come in just about every category, and since you've done your marketing homework, you already know the lists you want. The one-time rental fee for these names is between $35 and $50 per thousand, with a minimum rental of 5,000 names.

You can get more bang for your buck—or, to borrow those corporate buzzwords, "add value" to your direct mailer—by presenting some sort of bonus offer. Put something in the ad that will draw in new customers, perhaps a 20 percent discount or $10 coupon for the purchase of a studio package. This can be an excellent way to generate business.

Yellow Pages

Using directory advertising, such as the Yellow Pages of the local phone book, is a very important marketing tool that is often overlooked. Believe it or not, people actually

Make Contact with Coupons

If you're not feeling altogether flush, a viable direct-mail alternative is a coupon mailer that groups retail businesses within a community together in a bound coupon book, usually including advertisements, discounts, or special offers. The books are mailed nonselectively to all homes within a specific ZIP code, so they aren't as targeted as a direct-mail piece that you'd design yourself, but they can still have great pull. As a business owner, you pay a fee to the company producing and distributing the coupon books. These companies should be listed in your Yellow Pages.

use these tomes for more than doorstops and birdcage liners. When prospective customers are looking for specific products or services in the directory, they are excellent prospects because they are actively looking for a wedding, portrait, or commercial photographer.

Placing your listing under the right category is critical so people can find you. You will increase the chances of a potential client seeing your business name if you insert your listing under multiple headings or categories.

Business Cards

As small as they are, business cards are a powerful marketing tool. Hand out these little gems at every opportunity. Think of them as mini-billboards that tell people who you are, what you do, and how to reach you.

Whenever you meet someone—in church, at your kids' school, in the grocery store, waiting in lobbies, at business meetings, or anywhere else—and the subject of what you do for a living comes up, hand over your business card as you describe your company. As a matter of fact, give people two cards—one to keep and one to pass along to someone else.

A quick-print shop can do a nice, affordable job on your business cards by providing a variety of templates to choose from. You can also order them online from companies like Vista Print (www.vistaprint.com) for a nominal charge.

Press Releases

Press releases are free publicity spots that expose your business to the community; but to be printed in the newspaper, the information has to be newsworthy. One way this

Charitable Donations

Offer to donate portrait sitting packages or framed prints as charitable donations to silent auctions. This technique can be even more effective if an existing client is a member of that charity's organization and can help to promote your print or services.

At a parent's request, Jerry Clement contributed one of his popular gallery prints to a school auction a few years ago. The parent had decided in advance she was taking the framed print home with her, but at the auction, her enthusiasm was contagious and encouraged the bids of several other patrons. Not only did the print fetch a generous profit for the school, it also introduced some new clients to Clement.

subtle form of self-promotion can be done is by tying the announcement into local or national events, community programs, or holidays.

Make up a list of media contacts, including television, radio, newspaper, and community organizations, so that when you are ready, you can send out a press release blitz. Be sure to include your contact information, including your cell phone number. Folks in the media work on tight deadlines, and if they can't reach you right away to ask questions, they may be inclined to drop the story and move on.

Television/Radio

Television and radio can be effective in your marketing strategy if you're advertising something concrete, like a holiday promotion or a special event. It also helps if you're advertising locally, where you know potential customers are listening to your chosen station.

While these stations only reach very small geographic areas, their programs are specifically designed to appeal to the people in this limited market. When you buy time on a small radio or cable TV station, you're not paying for wasted circulation. Rates are usually pretty reasonable, and you can create your own interesting, affordable ad.

Magazine and Publication Ads

Magazine and publication ads seem to be only minimally effective for photographers. In addition, they are sometimes expensive and can be hard to get responses from unless they are carefully crafted with an explicit call to action. That's usually achieved by promoting a specific product, service, or information. Add an incentive such as a discount if a client contacts you and mentions seeing the advertisement, or include a coupon as part of your display ad.

Use niche publications that match your business. For instance, a commercial photographer can use architectural or interior design magazines. Advertising in local newspapers is another way to create public awareness of your business.

Web-Wise

Today, an internet presence is as essential as a telephone and fax machine. A web site is your online brochure, and it can be working for you 24 hours a day, seven days a week. In addition to credibility, a web site gives you a variety of marketing opportunities.

"A web site is basically how photographs are presented to prospective buyers these days," says Ray Strawbridge. "Wedding photographers no longer have to put together a 4x5 book of proofs for the bride and groom to run around and show Grandma and Aunt Nelly. Now they are posted on the web, and anyone with the link can take a look and place an order."

This is the same strategy that Carmen Davis uses for posting images taken at dog show events. "The day after a project, I get the pictures all ready and upload them to my web site," she says. "Everyone already knows to go to my site if they want to see their dogs and place an order. It's pretty standard in the dog show world, and it probably is with other photographic events. So this isn't breaking new ground or anything."

Whether you decide to set up and design your own web site or hire someone to do it for you, there are some things you need to think about in advance. The first and most important is registering a primary domain name. This is the first thing that pops up when someone is doing an online search for your business. The domain name of your web site should be the same as your business, if possible and practical. At the very least, it should reflect the nature of your services. It should also be 20 characters or fewer so it's easy for people to remember. Also, the fewer the characters, the less likely it is that someone will make a mistake typing the address into their browser.

Use a reliable web host provider. A web host stores your web site, including graphics, and transmits it to the internet for other users to view. Not all web hosts are created alike, so shop around for one that has the best package for your needs. Some will even include free domain registration, free design templates, or no setup fees.

To promote your web site, you will need to devise a separate marketing plan that should include:

- *Search engine submissions.* You can undertake this task yourself by submitting your web site to all the search engines (there are hundreds) or by hiring a marketing specialist to do this for you.

- *Reciprocal links.* Text or banner links are exchanged with another web site owner. Many search engines keep track of how many sites point back to your link. The more sites that promote your business, the higher visibility your web site will have when someone does a search.

- *Online newsletters or "ezines."* These are helpful marketing tools that you publish monthly or weekly. Interested parties subscribe to your newsletter to receive articles and informative tips from you. It puts your business's name in front of them on a regular basis.

- *Mini-sites.* There are a number of photography databases like PhotoServe (www.photoserve.com), Workbook (www.workbook.com) or Artist Registry (www.artistregistry.com) that allow registered members to upload some of their images and add a link to their web sites. "A lot of times this is where clients are looking these days," says Weschler.

Ira Gostin uses an e-mail list to let interested parties know when he has uploaded new images to his web site. "Instead of telling people 'Hey, go to my web site because I've got some new stuff,' I will send a link to the actual picture," he says. "Hopefully, they will be interested enough to browse around and look at some of my other pictures." Gostin says he can also track what pages visitors frequent the most on his site. "For example, I know that my Elvis picture story is the most popular page visited, and this helps me to know what images are getting the most exposure."

> **Smart Tip**
> Tip...
> Visit Nameboy.com (www.nameboy.com) to find clever and interesting domain names in your area of specialty. This great free nickname generator can be used for finding names for almost anything, although it is primarily used to find domain names for web sites. Simply type in two keywords that best describe your business and let Nameboy do the rest.

Portfolios

All of our featured photographers agreed that their respective web sites function as online portfolios and the internet is where the majority of clients and prospective buyers find them. "It's not unusual for someone to call me and say they looked at some of my prints online and would like to see some additional samples," says Ray Strawbridge. He used to take a light box with him to a client's office, along with another case that had a selection of 4x5 transparencies mounted on black mats. "It was kind of aggravating and cumbersome," he admits. "Fortunately, because of the digital age, most portfolios have gone to prints, which make it easier for everyone."

Michael Weschler has two portfolios: one that holds prints and another that has tear sheets. "I still present them upon request, but its not as often as before," he says. "I think most people are looking at the web site. Plus, you eventually become known for your work after a while."

Galleries and art shows typically request that images be submitted in a digital format, so Jerry Clement scans his pictures to be placed on a disk. However, his actual portfolio holds 11x14 representative samples that are placed on 16x20 mats. "It's difficult to look at a 5x7 snapshot of something and translate that into something that might hang on the wall," he says. "So I like to have my portfolio prints in the size that most people would relate to as a wall decoration."

> **Smart Tip** — Tip...
>
> E-mail signature lines are very important and need to be at the bottom of every message you send out. They should be made up of approximately four to five lines with your name, company name, web address, and services.

Art Shows and Galleries

A number of photographers make their living solely by exhibiting in major art shows and festivals while others may do it seasonally. It's not an easy process, requiring a lot of travel and the loss of your weekends, but it can be a rewarding one.

It's generally recommended that new art exhibitors start at local events sponsored by community groups, schools, and churches. Once you have some experience and are feeling comfortable exhibiting your work, you can move on to state and regional shows for more exposure. The bigger shows have bigger entry fees and more stringent requirements. For these shows, there are typically more applications than booths, and there is no guarantee you will be accepted. The best quality shows and festivals are juried by a panel of experts who determine who can participate from their applications and submitted slides, so make sure your submissions are your best work.

▲

Bright Idea

In addition to the framed photographs that are hung for display, also offer unframed images for sale. This gives you the opportunity to sell a less expensive item to budget-conscious consumers as well as to exhibit other images that might not be included in the booth's theme.

The Initial Process

Before applying to some of the better art shows, visit them first to see what other photographers are exhibiting and how they are displaying their work. Not just anyone can jury into an art show. The competition is fierce on two levels: first, for space to show your photographs; and secondly, for sales.

The application process usually starts months in advance and requires hopeful exhibitors to submit a biography or resume, the application, an application fee, a jury fee, jury slides, and sometimes a list of customers and marketing materials such as brochures or other publications.

You can find out about art shows and festivals from other exhibitors as well as through your local chamber of commerce. For information on regional and national shows, take a look at the *Art Fair Sourcebook* (www.artfairsource.com), which is put together annually by veteran art show photographer, Greg Lawler. Another useful publication is the *Sunshine Artist Magazine* (www.sunshineartist.com), which is an in-depth magazine for major art shows and festivals.

On the Circuit

Once you've been accepted to a show or festival, find out what will be provided and what you will need to bring. If the festival is taking place outdoors, exhibitors usually provide their own canopies, which can be purchased or rented. Whether you are exhibiting indoors or out, you will also need to provide display racks or fabric walls on which to hang your photographs. Other important considerations are incidentals like a comfortable chair, display tables, and bins.

Next, think about how you want to present your photographs to their best advantage. If there is a row of 150 booths, what do you have that will draw in browsers to look at your images? It's great if you have a "show stopper," but its even better if you have several of those to grab folks' interest and get them talking.

You also have to think about what photographs work well together as a unified body. It's not enough to simply throw a bunch of your favorite pictures together and hang them up. If buyers are looking at a wall featuring a wedding, a landscape, and a building design, they are going to be confused. Decide who you are marketing to and give those images the wall space they deserve. Keep in mind that your booth basically functions as a mini showroom, and an attractive set up helps customers visualize how a certain piece will look in their home or office.

Galleries

Several of our featured photographers have promoted their work in galleries, including Jerry Clement and Michael Weschler. Although Weschler no longer participates in gallery showings, this an ongoing business practice for Clement.

"It's pretty difficult getting into the better known galleries initially," says Clement. "One way to build your reputation is to approach new gallery owners who may be looking to represent unknown but talented artists."

The application process is very similar to applying for an art show: you submit the required paperwork (sometimes with a fee) by the registration deadline, along with copies of your work for approval (sometimes by a jury). Gallery images are typically displayed for up to a month, unless you are applying for permanent representation.

Unlike an art show, you are not required to be present at the gallery during operating hours, which takes a lot of pressure off the artist. If one of your images sells, gallery personnel handle everything from collecting the money to delivery of the product, while tucking away a commission for their part in closing the deal.

Trade Shows and Conferences

Trade shows and conferences can be a tremendous opportunity for learning—or a huge waste of time.

There are two types of shows: consumer, which focus on home, garden, and other consumer themes, and business-to-business, where exhibitors market their products and services to other companies. You can likely benefit by attending, and perhaps even exhibiting, in both.

For example, if you are a wedding photographer, consider exhibiting in a wedding show expo or a women's trade show like the Southern Women's Shows (www.southernshows.com). Commercial photographers can set up booths at building and remodeling expos such as the International Builders Show (www.buildersshow.com).

You can find trade shows scheduled throughout the country at *Tradeshow Week Online* (www.tradeshowweek.com) or *Tradeshow News Network* (www.tsnn.com).

Kill 'Em With Kindness

As we mentioned at the beginning of this chapter, you are your best marketing tool and nothing can beat good old-fashioned customer service. The internet has changed the face of photography and business in countless ways, but it still hasn't "changed everything," as we so often hear—certainly not when it comes to marketing.

That is the view, at least, of Kenneth Salzmann, a photojournalist and writer who began his career in the 1970s. "The internet can and does open many new doors," he says, "but what keeps them open is an old-fashioned commitment to customer satisfaction—the level of quality, responsiveness, integrity, and timeliness that makes today's client a repeat customer." Holding on to a client for the long run, he adds, is not only good for business, but also a good business practice in and of itself. "It costs more than meets the eye to lose a customer," Salzmann says.

Bright Idea

There are many ways that you can market your photography skills without being obtrusive. One amateur photographer put a couple of 5x7 prints in nondescript picture frames and hung them on her cubicle wall at work. Because they were of good quality and detail, visitors noticed them right away and asked questions about where they originated. She ended up selling several prints for $30 each and was commissioned by a co-worker to take pictures at her son's bar mitzvah.

Crunching the Numbers:
Finances and Taxes

T he best indicator of how serious you are about your photography business is how you handle the money. And if you're serious about your business, you need to be serious about the money. Basically, there are two sides to the issue of money: how much you need to start and operate, and how much you can expect to take in. Doing this type of research is often difficult for photographers who would rather be out in the field or in the studio doing their work than bound to a desk dealing with tiresome numbers. But to be successful, you're going to have to force yourself to do it anyway.

Start-Up Funds

As noted earlier, many photographers start out part time and eventually segue into a full-time business as time and money permit. This gives entrepreneurs the opportunity to generate sufficient income to cover expenses and make a profit without borrowing a big chunk of change—at least initially. Although it's easy to spend thousands of dollars starting a new business, with clever financial planning, you could operate with an investment of just a few hundred dollars.

Smart Tip

Ira Gostin says before starting a new business venture, you should first have some capital in the bank. "The rule of thumb is to have three months saved for mortgage/rent payments, car payments, and life money (food, utilities, etc.)," he cautions. "You should also have enough capital set aside to buy whatever equipment you are going to need."

How much money you need in the beginning depends on a number of factors, such as whether you will be homebased or in a commercial studio. Or whether you will have to upgrade your facilities and get more sophisticated equipment. Other considerations are inventory, supplies, licenses, permits, marketing, and operating capital needs (the amount of cash you need on hand to carry you until your business begins generating income). Use the Start-Up Costs Worksheet on page 92 to estimate how much money you're going to need.

So where is the money? Take a look at the following suggestions for some ideas:

- *Personal resources.* When thinking of creative ways to come up with start-up funds, do a thorough inventory of your own assets. Make a list of what you have, including savings and retirement accounts, equity in real estate, vehicles, collections, life insurance and other investments. Though you may not want to sell your car or siphon funds from your retirement account to finance your photography business, you may be willing to sell that vintage Seiki Canon camera for a few thousand dollars. It's just collecting dust anyway. But if you don't want to sell your assets for cash, think about using them as collateral for a loan.

- *Credit cards.* Many successful businesses have been jump-started with plastic. Just be smart about it because sky-high interest rates could bury you for years. If you do use a credit card to help fund your photography business, only charge items that will contribute to revenue generation. For example, upgrading to new and improved digital photo batching tools is an enormous timesaver when you have thousands of images to edit, making it an acceptable item to charge.

- *Friends and family.* A lot of start-up businesses have been funded with seed money from friends and relatives who recognized the potential value of the venture and wanted to help their loved ones succeed. However, be cautious with these arrangements; no matter how close you are, present yourself professionally, put everything in writing, and be sure the individuals you approach can afford to take the risk of investing in your business. Never accept money for a business venture from anyone who can't afford to lose that money.

- *Partners.* Using the "strength in numbers" principle, look around for someone who may want to team up with you in your venture. You may choose someone who has financial resources and wants to work side-by-side with you in the business. Or you may find someone who has money to invest but no interest in doing the actual work. As with your friends and family, be sure to create a written partnership agreement that clearly defines your respective responsibilities and obligations.

- *Government programs.* Take advantage of the abundance of local, state, and federal programs designed to support small businesses. Make your first stop the SBA; then investigate various other programs. Women, minorities, and veterans should check out niche financing possibilities designed to help them get into business. The business section of your local library is a good place to begin your research.

- *Lending institutions.* While banks might seem like the most likely sources of financing, they are generally the most conservative (something about wanting to hang onto their money). Besides wanting to know exactly what the money is for (show them your business plan), they usually require some type of collateral such as real estate, a life insurance policy, stocks, bonds, or a savings account. If you have excellent credit, you may be able to take out a signature loan for a few thousand dollars, although the interest rate will be higher than a traditional loan.

▲

Start-Up Costs Worksheet

Expenses

Mortgage/Rent _____

Utility deposits _____

Upgrade/Remodeling _____

Photography equipment _____

Office equipment _____

Supplies/Materials _____

Licenses/Permits _____

Accounting/Legal fees _____

Advertising/Marketing _____

Vehicle _____

Owner/Operator salary _____

Payroll _____

Insurance (first quarter) _____

Miscellaneous _____

_____

_____

_____

_____

TOTAL _____

Financial Management

It's important to monitor your financial progress closely, and the only way you can do that is by keeping good records. You can handle the process manually; however, there are a number of excellent computer accounting programs on the market.

Whatever accounting system you use will help produce financial statements that tell you exactly where you stand and what you need to do next. The key financial statements you need to understand and use regularly are:

- *Profit and loss statement* (also called the *P&L* or the *income statement*). This statement illustrates how much your business is making or losing over a designated period—monthly, quarterly, or annually—by subtracting expenses from your revenue to arrive at a net result, which is either a profit or a loss. Initially, this document may not be of much value to you—especially during the start-up phase. But over time as your profit history grows, you will appreciate this useful management tool.

- *Balance sheet.* A balance sheet is a table showing your assets, liabilities, and capital at a specific point. A balance sheet is typically generated monthly, quarterly, or annually when the books are closed.

- *Cash flow statement.* This summarizes the operating, investing, and financing activities of your business as they relate to the inflow and outflow of cash. Its main purpose is to point out when the cash flow isn't flowing so you can work out a solution and pinpoint trouble spots in the future. As with the profit and loss statement, a cash flow statement is prepared to reflect a specific accounting period, such as monthly, quarterly, or annually.

Successful business owners review these reports regularly, at least monthly, so they always know where they stand and can quickly move to correct minor difficulties before they become major financial problems. If you wait until June to figure out whether or not you made a profit last December, you will not be in business very long.

Once you have a fiscal system in place, your next step is to open a separate checking account for your business so that you don't commingle personal and business funds. You will also need a business credit card or at least a separate card in your name that you use exclusively for your photography business.

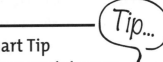

Smart Tip

If you carry a balance on a credit card that is used solely for business purposes, the interest is deductible, but if you mix business and personal charges on the card, the interest is not even partially deductible.

Taxing Matters

Businesses are required to pay a wide range of taxes. Not to sound like a broken record, but *keep good records* so you can offset your local, state, and federal income taxes with the expenses of operating your company.

If you have employees, you'll be responsible for payroll taxes. If you operate as a corporation, you'll have to pay payroll taxes for yourself; as a sole proprietor, you'll pay self-employment tax. Then there are property taxes, taxes on your equipment and inventory, fees and taxes to maintain your corporate status, your business license fee (which is really a tax), and other lesser-known taxes.

You must report all income from your photography business, no matter how insignificant. Failing to do so is a crime. If a government bean counter starts pouring over your books, a defense of "I didn't think you would catch me" isn't going to be much value if you are caught not reporting income. And just so you know, many financial institutions report to the IRS how much nonemployment money individuals deposit in their accounts.

Of course, in addition to reporting all your income, you should take every single deduction to which you are legally entitled. Homebased businesses may qualify for the home office deduction, which allows you to deduct a portion of your rent, mortgage interest, household utilities and services, real estate taxes, homeowners insurance, repairs, security systems, and depreciation. If you're driving back and forth to the post office or go on other business-related errands, you can either deduct mileage or depreciate your car and write off the actual expenses.

Also, be sure you charge, collect, and remit appropriate sales tax on your products and services. To do this, you'll need a sales tax ID number, which you can usually get by simply filling out a form. Check with your state's department of revenue for information on how to get a tax ID number.

Finally, take the time to review all your tax liabilities with your accountant.

How Will You Get Paid?

An important part of financial management is setting up an easy-to-manage account receivables system. This includes establishing clear and appropriate policies that are fair to your clients and protect you.

As part of their billing practices, many photographers extend credit by systematically

Tip...

Smart Tip
Use your invoices as marketing tools. Add a brochure or promotional flier to the envelope. Even though the invoice is going to an existing client, you never know where your brochures will end up.

generating invoices or monthly statements. This task can be easily handled with bookkeeping software programs like QuickBooks that include a basic invoicing function. However, if you choose to design your own invoices and statements, be sure they're clear and easy to understand. Detail each item, and indicate the amount due in bold with the words "Please pay" in front of the total. A confusing invoice may be set aside for clarification, and your payment will be delayed.

Decide when payments are due, and make that a clear part of your policy statement. Your policy should also address how far an account may be in arrears before you suspend services to that client until full payment is made. This is always a tough call, but remember that you are a for-profit business, and if you don't get paid, you can't pay your own bills and make a profit.

Accepting Credit and Debit Cards

Whether for convenience, security, reward points, or out of habit, many of today's consumers prefer to pay with plastic. Most small-business owners find it helps if they are able to accept credit and debit cards. Fortunately, it's much easier to get merchant status than it has been in the past; in fact, these days merchant status providers are competing aggressively for your business.

To get a credit card merchant account, start with your own bank. Also, check with various professional associations that offer merchant status as a member benefit. Shop around; this is a competitive industry, and it's worth taking the time to get the best deal.

Accepting Checks

Although paying by plastic is a popular trend, many of your clients will prefer to write you a check. Businesses lose more than $1 billion annually because of bad checks, so look for several key items when accepting them.

Check the date for accuracy. Do not accept a check that is undated, postdated, or more than 30 days old. Be sure the written amount and numerical amount agree. Post your check acceptance procedures in a highly visible place at your studio, or in your contract or agreement. This listing should also include the steps you will take if a check is returned for nonpayment. Most clients understand the risks you take when accepting checks and will be willing to follow your rules.

What's in the Forecast?

You don't need a crystal ball to predict future revenue, but you do need a formula to foresee how much you can expect to make in the weeks, months, and years ahead, as these numbers will become your sales goals. Pay close attention to and utilize your key financial statements on a routine basis. Plan for the costs of growth and watch for signs of developing problems so you can figure out how to best deal with them before they turn into a major crisis. Developing analytical foresight demonstrates that you are an astute business owner on top of every situation.

The Price is Right:
Knowing the Value of Your Art

Being a professional photographer is one-half creative visual artist and one-half astute businessperson. It also means being your own product. Clients are under the impression when they purchase your photographs, they are buying an image or product. But in reality, they are acquiring your experience, expertise, creative vision, and understanding of the assignment neatly packaged in a 5x7-inch proof. In essence, your services are your product. So how do you sell that great product? That's what we're going to discuss in this chapter.

A lot of variables come into play when trying to establish fees and rates for your photography business. Two of the most significant considerations are your specialty and geographical location. An event photographer's fees are predictably higher in Seattle, Washington, than Madison, Wisconsin, due to the cost of living factor. On the other hand, the event photographer in Madison will most likely have a more thriving business than a fashion photographer in the same area because of better opportunities. However, if the fashion photographer were willing to travel to metropolitan areas like Seattle, the event photographer would probably be left crying in the dust. Lots of variables.

Determining a feasible pricing structure is one of the most daunting tasks a new photography entrepreneur faces. There's not a magic formula when deciding how much to charge for your work, but hopefully we can provide some helpful guidelines.

Pricing Strategies

In a world of easy, digital imaging for the masses, photographers are finding new challenges when it comes to getting a fair price for their work, but instead of giving up the game, they should "change some of the rules," says one industry expert in a 2007 article for Wedding and Portrait Photographers International and *Rangefinder* magazine. Kirsten Carey, an author and consultant for the business side of creative work, noted that digital media are making it harder to charge for prints in the traditional way. So rather than a "nickel and dime" pricing strategy, she suggests photographers should charge for what clients really value—the ability to capture moments. "Start charging for what the client really values and you will see an increase in revenue and an increase in high-paying clients," she says.

A photographer's estimate is usually based on two elements: creative fees and expenses. On the creative side, you need to think about the quality of the image and what value you place on it. Jerry Clement says his formula for gallery prints includes the cost of production and what he calls an "intrinsic, artistic value," with some profit margin on top of that. "You also have to

> **Tip...**
>
> ## Smart Tip
> Use the price point appeal psychology to capture potential customers. For whatever reason, a $49.99 portrait sitting fee sounds so much better than $50. And discounts rounded to even numbers like 10 or 20 percent seem to work better than odd figures like 15 percent; perhaps because it's easier to do the math.

Cradoc fotoSoftware (www.fotoquote.com) is one of several software programs available to help freelance photographers with pricing strategies. Using a database of statistical pricing information, you can estimate appropriate fees for a specific project by keying in numerous factors.

take in account the gallery's commission which usually averages 30–40 percent," he says.

As part of your fees, you will also need to factor in labor, supplies, and materials. Will the images be shot on location or in a studio? If you are operating a studio, take a long hard look at your local competitors to see what they are charging for similar services and then start your pricing somewhere in the middle.

Wedding, portrait, and event photographers have an easier time scoping out the competition because it's easy to stop by and pick up a price list and other information. And although its simple enough to pick up the phone and call a commercial photographer about their fees, its highly unlikely you will get a standard rate because fees are usually developed on a project-by-project basis. Commercial photographer Ray Strawbridge says that new clients usually want to know what everything is going to cost before you ever do anything. "And until you do it, you don't really know," he says. "But if you have to speculate on a project and you're not a complete idiot, you're going to pad it because you never know what you're going to run into."

This will be a wobbly balancing act in the beginning until you have a handle on pricing formulas. You don't want to have the most expensive gig in town, but neither

Do the Math

When a CBS *Market Watch* report included wedding photographers in a list of "the ten most overpaid jobs in the U.S.," industry leaders were quick to respond with a barrage of facts and figures meant to set the record straight. The journalist was counting money that never makes it to the photographers' pockets, according to officials from the Professional Photographers of America, citing studies that show that more than 70 percent of the fees paid to wedding photographers go toward overhead.

If a photographer were to shoot 40 weddings a year at an average price of $4,000—well above the $1,750 norm of the time—that still would mean a salary just of about $48,000 out of gross revenues of $160,000, photographer and PPA officer Ann Monteith wrote to the reporter in a letter posted on the organization's web site. In fact, the average wedding photographer of the time, she said, worked 45 hours a week and made less than $25,000 a year.

do you want to run bargain-basement specials. People have a habit of equating quality with cost, but they also like getting a good deal. See what we mean about a balancing act? In essence, you want there to be a higher perceived value without pricing yourself out of the market.

Location shoots are more complex and involve considerations like site logistics, travel, special equipment or props, and additional personnel (e.g., models, assistants, technicians). In addition to the complexity of the project, the photographer also needs to take into account the number of finished images needed, scheduling, and pre- and post-production time.

Pre-production responsibilities may include client meetings, site location, and/or visits and set arrangements. After the shoot is over, post-production tasks may consist of restoring a site to its original state, returning props and equipment, and more client meetings—along with editing, selecting, and finalizing the images.

Many commercial or location photographers charge day or half-day rates, with rates adjusted to weekly for long-term shoots or hourly for shorter projects. Don't forget to add overtime (hourly rate plus 50 percent) for days that go longer than eight hours or for weekend assignments.

Whenever in doubt, use the industry standards found through different photography associations and organizations like American Society for Media Photographers (ASMP) or Professional Photographers of America (PPA). Local chapters have monthly meetings where members can network and find out a wealth of information, including marketing and industry standards in your area.

Usage Fees

A usage fee is what a photographer charges based on how the image(s) will be used by the client. Strawbridge says that the ASMP and Advertising Photographers of America (APA) encourage photographers toward a usage sort of model. But he thinks that's more of a goal and not necessarily a reality—at least in the smaller market places like where he lives. "It really depends on the client," Strawbridge says. "I have done some things with national agencies and had some extremely lucrative usage fees. But when I do similar work for local clients, I pretty much charge by the hour, plus the number of prints. I may also charge them a little extra to use an image on their web site."

Strawbridge deviates from the usage model for local clients who sometimes have a difficult time understanding the concept. "You can give someone an analogy about not loading Microsoft

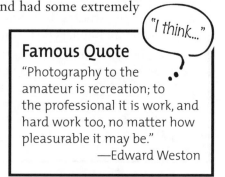

Famous Quote

"Photography to the amateur is recreation; to the professional it is work, and hard work too, no matter how pleasurable it may be."
—Edward Weston

"I think..."

> **Tip...**
>
> **Smart Tip**
>
> After factoring your costs into your pricing structure, find ways to reduce those costs and increase profits. Monitor your progress each month by utilizing Profit and Loss Reports (see page 104).

software on a dozen different computers, but they just don't want to hear it," he says. "All they know is they paid you to shoot this picture and now you're saying they don't own it. It can be frustrating and sometimes it's just better not to go there, especially if the client is not going to use the image more than once beyond the local market. So I just try to keep the image file out of their hands as much as possible."

However, note that the usage fee model works quite well in larger, metropolitan cities like New York City, Los Angeles, Reno, and Seattle, as Michael Weschler and Ira Gostin will attest.

"A lot of photographers have trouble understanding the value of their work in the beginning," says Weschler. "But it's important to protect your intellectual property. If someone wants to pay you $500 for an image but they want all rights, you can end up selling yourself short. If it's a really good image that you can resell each time the embargo period ends, you might make $5,000 on it instead."

The usage fee model is also used when working with stock agencies. Ideally, you will be affiliated with a reputable agency that will sometimes tell you who the client is. Even if they don't, they will still give you the parameters of how the image will be used. Ray Strawbridge sums it up like this: "If it's a stock image you own and can license to somebody simply for usage like an editorial publication, then that is pretty cut and dried. If they put it on the front cover its one fee, if they put a quarter page inside the magazine it's another fee," he says. "The fee is based on the circulation of the magazine, the size and position it will be used. The more times they are going to use it, the more insertions and the larger circulation of the publication, then the more that image is worth."

Ira Gostin says that one of the misconceptions that many people have is that photographers sell pictures. "We don't. We license usage," he says. "That means keeping track of your images and how clients are using them."

Expenses

The other part of the pricing equation is expenses. Many photographers—especially in the beginning—try to absorb minor expenses like supplies, postage, and film. But these little things quickly add up and chip away at your profits. Your fee structure should cover these incidentals. For example, if you decide $50 is a fair hourly rate—charge $60. Then use the hourly charge to calculate daily and weekly rates.

Overhead should also be a calculated expense that includes rent, utilities, insurance, gas, mileage, and anything else that you are not billing clients separately for. Big

▲

Stock Photography Usage Fee Pricing

There are a lot of factors when determining an appropriate usage fee. Things that you need to find out include:

- How will the image be used? Editorial, advertising, corporate, web site?

- What type of publication? Print ad, brochure, billboard, electronic (web site, banner ad)?

- What is the circulation? Local, regional, national, World Wide Web?

- What size will the image be? If print, will it be a cover page, half page, quarter page? If electronic, will be on the home page or a secondary page?

- How long does the client want to hold exclusive rights to this image? This can range anywhere from a one-time, nonexclusive use to a specified period—sometimes even unlimited use.

- How will the selected image(s) be delivered: Transparency or digital file? Hand delivered, shipped, e-mailed?

Other factors that may have an effect on usage fees are:

- Photographer's minimum fee
- Production costs
- Site location and preparation
- Uniqueness of image
- Special equipment
- Additional risk factors

ticket expenses for individual assignments like travel, equipment, or personnel should be billed separately, depending on your—or the client's—preferences.

Photographers often go into the profession out of a love for the art or science of it; but sometimes they overlook a basic business imperative, according to a host of industry experts who have made "Cost of Doing Business" (CODB) a key part of the advice they offer. Mark Loundy, writing on *Return to Common Cents* (www.loundy.org/commoncents), reminded his readers in a 2006 article that, "If you don't include your own pay in your CODB, you're missing the whole point." Rather than paying yourself "what's left over," pay yourself first and view the rest of your costs as overhead, he advises. "If you don't have enough to make your own payroll, you'll have to either increase revenue or cut costs."

Deposits

A good business practice is to collect an advance deposit before starting a project. Traditionally, 50 percent is collected before commencement of the assignment, with the balance due upon completion. Of course, there are exceptions depending on your specialty. A wedding photographer usually collects a nonrefundable retainer of 25 percent or less, with the balance due before the wedding date. The photographer may also set up a payment schedule so the balance can be paid down in increments.

Bids and Estimates

It's important to understand the difference between placing a bid on a project and giving an estimate. A bid indicates that you are willing to do the assignment for a set price, whereas an estimate indicates how much you think a project will cost and allows for wiggle room.

Just for fun, let's say that a photographer in Spokane, Washington, is commissioned to photograph a client's champion quarter horse at an equestrian event in Salem, Oregon. The horse show takes place over a three-day span, but the photographer feels confident that he can get the requisite images in just one day. The photographer provides a bid for $2,195 that includes a full day rate ($1,500), four rolls of film ($200), and travel expenses ($495).

In one scenario, the weather is inclement during the first two days of the show and the photographer has to stay an extra night incurring additional expenses. Plus, he uses three extra rolls of film trying to capture that elusive shot. Unfortunately, the photographer loses money on this assignment.

But in another (better) scenario, the weather is fabulous and the photographer gets all the shots he needs in just half a day. Instead of staying overnight in Salem, he travels back to Spokane before nightfall saving on travel expenses and making a little extra on this assignment.

If the photographer had given an estimate on this project, he would have been able to bill the client for the additional time and expenses for the bad weather scenario. Or on the flip side, he could have saved the client some money and surprised her with a reduced invoice.

It's a tricky process, but whatever your approach is, take Ray Strawbridge's advice and don't be short sighted—pad that proposal because you don't know what's around the corner.

Profit & Loss Quarterly Report

INCOME	Jan	Feb	Mar	Qtr
Services	$_____	$_____	$_____	$_____
Product sales	$_____	$_____	$_____	$_____
Gross profit	$_____	$_____	$_____	$_____

EXPENSES	Jan	Feb	Mar	Qtr
Rent/Mortgage	$_____	$_____	$_____	$_____
Utilities	$_____	$_____	$_____	$_____
Phone (Cell/Office/Fax)	$_____	$_____	$_____	$_____
Equipment	$_____	$_____	$_____	$_____
Computer	$_____	$_____	$_____	$_____
Insurance	$_____	$_____	$_____	$_____
Vehicle	$_____	$_____	$_____	$_____
Travel	$_____	$_____	$_____	$_____
Taxes/Licenses	$_____	$_____	$_____	$_____
Payroll/Benefits	$_____	$_____	$_____	$_____
Advertising	$_____	$_____	$_____	$_____
Repairs/Maintenance	$_____	$_____	$_____	$_____
Legal/Accounting	$_____	$_____	$_____	$_____
Photography Supplies	$_____	$_____	$_____	$_____
Office Supplies	$_____	$_____	$_____	$_____
Professional Development	$_____	$_____	$_____	$_____
Postage/Shipping	$_____	$_____	$_____	$_____
Printing/Copying	$_____	$_____	$_____	$_____
Internet Service	$_____	$_____	$_____	$_____
Web Hosting	$_____	$_____	$_____	$_____
Miscellaneous	$_____	$_____	$_____	$_____
Total Expenses	$_____	$_____	$_____	$_____
Gross Net Profit (Loss)	$_____	$_____	$_____	$_____
Taxes	$_____	$_____	$_____	$_____

Net Profit (Loss) After Taxes $_____ $_____ $_____ $_____

Photographer Beware: Legal Issues in the Industry

Before stepping out into the scary world of business, it's important to understand some of the legal concerns that photographers might be faced with and what remedies are available. Otherwise, you might be left vulnerable to personal or professional liability, loss of income, and damage to your reputation.

Copyright Issues

A photographer owns the copyright to his images from the moment of creation according to the Copyright Act of 1976. Once you click the shutter, you are the creator and copyright owner without having to register it. This means if unauthorized use of an image occurs (and it frequently does), the photographer could be entitled to compensation. However, if its not registered and someone uses it without permission, the only thing you can collect are usage fees. If the image was grossly infringed upon and you feel entitled to additional compensation, including attorney's fees, you will not be able to collect punitive damages without a copyright registration.

People who blatantly infringe upon copyrights know this. They know the cost of pursing a settlement could be cost prohibitive, so there continues to be a tremendous benefit to registering your images for copyright protection. Michael Weschler says this is why he has started registering most of his images with the Library of Congress. "I want to protect my images, so I will send a disk with a collection of images to the Copyright Office." Visit the Library of Congress, Copyright Office (www.loc.gov /copyright) for instructions and guidelines on how to proceed.

Handle with Care

The reality is infringements are going to happen, but in most cases it comes from the infringer's simply not knowing the rules attached to usage rights. If you find someone who is using an image without authorization, it's important to handle the situation professionally. "Try to have good karma and serendipity," advises Ira Gostin. "When you see a photograph that is being used without your permission, contact that client or person and work it out."

Stat Fact
Copyrights have a pretty long shelf life. Any work that was copyrighted on or after January 1, 1978 is protected from the date of creation until 50 years after the creator dies. Once a copyright expires, the work (or image) becomes public domain and anyone can freely use it.

Weschler agrees sticky situations like these are best resolved professionally. "It's important to protect your intellectual property, but don't be hostile," he cautions. "Instead let the person know that your work has value, this is your baby and you've got to charge them for it. Then figure out a reasonable usage fee."

Weschler relates a scenario involving one of his images that was printed without permission on the cover of a trade magazine: "My studio manager found out about it by doing a routine Google® search. A client had given someone at the magazine a copy of the picture without realizing they needed to pay a fee and get permission. So we explained that the architect didn't own the image—I did. My rep handled it for me and was able to amicably work it out and determine an appropriate usage fee."

Protective Measures

Although using a copyright notice on your photographs is no longer necessary to safeguard your work from copyright infringement, doing so may still be a good idea, in the view of the National Press Photographers Association. As you know, under current law your work is copyrighted as soon as it is created, but using a copyright notice (©) may be important because it informs the public that the work is protected by copyright, identifies the copyright owner, and shows the year of first publication. Furthermore, in the event that a work is infringed, if a proper notice of copyright appears on the work [it can help establish the facts]," the NPPA says in an article on its web site, www.nppa.org, which contains a wealth of business and legal information.

Carmen Davis says that copyright infringement is a huge issue when it comes to the internet. "I've had my pictures show up all over the World Wide Web," she says. "Even on an AKC site in Turkey." She said she doesn't mind if other web site owners want to use her images, but they need to tell readers who the photographer is and provide a link. What she and many other photographers do now is put a watermark on the image to establish ownership.

Most photographers also upload images with low resolutions. This insures that the picture will be of poor, grainy quality if someone tries to blow it up and print it. Weschler also embeds identifiable meta-data in each image so that if it ends up in the wrong hands he has a digital paper trail—even if they copy it. As an added measure of protection, Gostin has included a script on his web site so that if someone attempts to right-click and copy one of his images, a friendly reminder pops up to let people know they need to ask for permission first. Here is an example:

> ### Bright Idea
> Michael Weschler recommends signing up for Google Alerts® (www.google.com/alerts) so that you are notified whenever an image is posted or your name is mentioned online. "It's great because I know when new things are published, which makes me happy to see that I'm getting some new press or exposure," he says.

When Do You Need Permission?

Technically, you can shoot anybody or anything you want on public property so long as its used in an editorial way and you are informing people about something that is a matter of public interest. Of course, there are exceptions to this rule, such as private events, and Ira Gostin paints an interesting (and fictional) scenario as an example:

"Let's say you are going to a San Francisco 49ers football game. You've got your backpack, lunch, camera, and 400 mm lens. First of all, you would never make it through the gate because you can't bring in cameras with detachable lenses—but let's assume you get away with it. You shoot some pictures and snag a really great shot that you print out and show to your friends and hang on your wall. That's all fine and dandy, until you get the great idea to put it on some t-shirts and sell them for a few dollars. Now you've got problems.

"Although the game was held in a public place, it was a licensed event, and you can't sell that image without permission from the team and the NFL. This is why photographers have to have press credentials. The teams and NFL monitor all the lights, logos, images, color schemes, and anything else that is considered proprietary information. That is the difference between taking and making photos. It shouldn't be a taking thing. There should be a conversation about it."

If you're going to use an image commercially such as promotional advertising, you're going to need to obtain all the proper releases. Weschler says that he *always* gets model and property releases and provides us with another example of why you should consider doing the same:

"If you're doing an editorial piece on vegetarians and snap a picture of someone eating asparagus soup, you don't need their permission. The gray area is if the magazine decides to use that image on its subscription cards, which is technically in an advertising capacity. The individual could come after you and say, 'Hey, I'm not promoting this magazine. I don't want to be a *Vegetarian News* poster child—I just thought I was part of a story about vegetarians.'"

You should always be aware of potential problems when shooting other people. No matter what kinds of limitations and disclaimers you attach to that image, you may not always have control of how it will be used in the hands of someone else. It's better to be safe than sorry and obtain the proper releases. Take a look at the sample model release form on page 109.

Sample Model Release Form

Name of Photographer: _____

Address: _____

_____

Phone: _____

Today's Date: _____

Description of Assignment: _____

_____

_____

Location: _____

_____

For valuable consideration received, I hereby grant the above photographer to use, reproduce, sell, and resell any pictures taken on this day of me, to be used for advertising, art, trade, publishing, or any other lawful purpose.

I further waive the right to inspect or approve these images or text that may be used in connection with them. All negatives and positives, together with the prints, shall constitute the photographer's sole property.

I am 18 years or older: Yes ____   No* ____

Model's Name (print): _____

Address: _____

Phone: _____

Signature of Model: _____

*Form must be signed by parent or legal guardian if model is under the age of 18.

Signature of Parent/Guardian: _____

Get It in Writing

You know that, right? This is simply good business practice and it doesn't have to be incomprehensible legal mumbo jumbo. Every business agreement should be documented in writing and photography assignments are no exception. While the word "contract" may sound intimidating, this does not have to be a complicated process. However, it does need to clearly address any and all issues relevant to the proposed assignment. Terms and conditions may vary from one project to the next, but the following topics should always be considered:

- *Assignment.* Provide a detailed description of what the assignment consists of. Are these editorial images to be used in publications, a commercial assignment to promote a client's products or services, or an event such as a wedding or bar mitzvah?

- *Duration.* The contract should state the exact date(s) this assignment should take place. Is this a one-day event, is the assignment expected to cover several days, or is this an ongoing project?

- *Location.* Has the location been predetermined or will the photographer need to research and scout for appropriate sites, venues, or surroundings? If the latter, the photographer will need to bill the client for the additional time involved.

- *Additional equipment, props, or models.* Many shoots require the use of professional models or special props and equipment. If the photographer is responsible for obtaining these, then the client should be billed separately.

- *Copyright/Ownership.* Unless this is a work-for-hire assignment, photographers generally retain the rights to their images while granting limited usage to the client.

- *Fees.* Fees will differ from one assignment to the next. How to determine fees is discussed in Chapter 12. In the contract, be sure to stipulate when payment is expected (e.g., upon receipt of invoice or 30 days after receipt) and if there will be a late-fee penalty. Attach a fee schedule for the client's use.

- *Deposits.* Depending on the scope of the project, advance deposits may be required in the amount of 25–50 percent. Specify in the contract what portions are non-refundable and when the final balance is due. For example, a wedding photographer usually requires the balance to be paid in full before showing up at the church, whereas a commercial photographer will not invoice the client until after the project has been completed.

- *Travel and expenses.* The client is responsible for any expenses incurred by the photographer during the commission of this assignment including hotel, rental car, airfare, mileage, equipment, etc. If the photographer anticipates the expenses to be significant, he or she can require the client to pay them in advance or obtain a deposit to be applied toward the estimated expenses.

- *Creative Judgment.* Typically, an authorized representative of the client will be present at a shoot to answer questions and instruct the photographer regarding the desired images. In the event a designated individual is not available, then add a clause to the contract stipulating that the client must accept the photographer's judgment in the creation of the images.

- *Completion Date.* State when the client can expect to have the desired images in hand.

- *Rescheduling/Changes to Assignment.* Sometimes an assignment needs to be rescheduled or changed for a variety of reasons. Specify what additional fees will be incurred, including any expenses related to the change.

- *Cancellations.* Clearly spell out in the contract what the client is responsible for in the event of a cancellation. Will all or a portion of the advance deposit be withheld? How many days can a client give notice of cancellation before additional fees are imposed? Usually the closer to the scheduled date, the higher the penalty. Don't forget to include charges for any expenses that have been incurred.

- *Liability.* There should be a clause in the contract that holds the photographer harmless against any claims, liability, or damages that could arise from the client's misuse of the images.

- *Previews.* If the client is given proofs or previews to review, make sure they understand these images are the property of the photographer unless stated otherwise. To encourage compliance, insert a clause that states a standard fee will charged unless the photographs are returned in X number of days (usually 30–45).

> **Tip...**
>
> **Smart Tip**
>
> The American Society of Media Photographers (www.asmp.org) has sample contracts, agreements, and other useful forms available for its members on their web site. You can also find some standardized forms at your local office supply store.

Truisms: What You Won't See Through the Eye of the Camera

By now, you should know how to get started and have a good idea of what to do—and what not to do—in your own photography business. But nothing teaches as well as the voice of experience. So we asked our featured photographers to tell us what else has contributed to their success. Here's what they had to say.

Be Prepared!

This was a sentiment echoed by every photographer we spoke to. Jerry Clement said he learned his first lesson about being prepared as a photographer at the young age of 12. A couple he knew was getting married in a simple ceremony and had asked him to take pictures at the wedding. He was very excited about his first photographic opportunity, but neglected to check everything beforehand. "I had everything set up and was ready to go when I discovered my flash didn't work," Clement says. "The only pictures I was able to take were outside, so I was downtrodden. Now, I double-check everything!"

Michael Weschler says he takes two or three of everything with him on location shoots. "I'm not a worrywart, but I make it a point to plan for the worst and hope for the best," he says. "You don't want to be in a situation where you have to cancel a shoot because your camera or some other piece of equipment isn't working. Things fail, stuff breaks and if you're on an island in Hawaii, insurance isn't going to bail you out. People schedule their lives around shoots and everyone is going to be upset, so it pays to be prepared."

Don't Quit Your Day Job

This sage advice comes from Ray Strawbridge, who says there are going to be peaks and valleys in the photography business—especially when you're just starting out. "Photography can be very profitable, but it's difficult for any small business owner," he says. "You have to be very disciplined and very dedicated. If you are not working on an assignment, then you should be out beating the bushes. Sometimes you can make as much in a day doing photography as you can in a week doing something else. But if you're not busy every day and you're trying to do this for a living, you better have another job to go to until you're up and running."

Quality Prints Without a Printer

As a part-time photographer, Carmen Davis was not willing to invest in an expensive, high-quality printer, so she set out to find an alternative. What she discovered was the Kodak Gallery (www.kodakgallery.com), which could provide top-quality prints for pennies apiece. "Prints from a home digital printer have a 5–7 year shelf life, but if someone buys a picture from me, I want them to have it for 20 years or more," she says. "Kodak was able to match the quality I was looking for in a variety of sizes at a very reasonable price."

Images are uploaded to the Kodak Gallery's web site, then are printed out and shipped to the recipient. If this is a rush delivery, prints can be picked up the same day at a local participating retailer—for an additional fee, of course. Otherwise, overnight shipping is available.

Get Smart

We've stressed the power of knowledge throughout the book, and we're going to push it one more time. "There are a lot of things photographers don't know about but could learn by going to seminars," says Ira Gostin. "There's a lot of information for a beginning photographer, such as legal information, how to set up a business, learn about digital imaging, etc." Many seminars and workshops are offered through various photography associations and organizations. You can find out about some of these in the Appendix. Another smart thing is to join one of these associations so you can network and learn from your peers who have been there and done that.

Excellent Business Tips

Ira Gostin is very active with the American Society of Media Photographers and he has written a number of educational articles for the ASMP that can be found on its web site. Gostin gave us permission to reprint this excerpt from one of his articles.

1. *Be in Business.* If you are going to be in business, then be in business. The business side of freelancing is as important as making great photographs. Learn the skills you need, assemble a support team, and know where your resources are.

2. *Be Professional.* Always remember that when you are working for any given client, they are the center of your universe. Be prompt, polite, well mannered, a business professional.

3. *Know the Law.* Take time to find out the specific business laws of your community. Business licenses, sales tax and resale laws, and liability insurance are just a few things that are extremely important.

4. *Personal Time.* Allow yourself some time to relax, exercise, get fresh air, and in general, just wind down a little and recharge. Schedule this time as you would an appointment so you are sure to do it!

5. *Plan, Plan, Plan.* A business plan is instrumental in keeping your business on track. It does not need to be some multi-volume document with hundreds of

▲

footnotes. Just a simple outline with your goals and strategies clearly outlined will keep you on track.

6. *Be Portfolio Honest.* Your portfolio should display your images in a professional fashion that is easy to look at and conveys a bit of your personality as well. Your promo materials should always reflect the type of work you do. If you do not own strobes, don't show a lot of lit images that you are not able to create on a regular basis.

7. *Learn & Associate.* Attend workshops, seminars, and association meetings. Plan at least a one-day seminar every quarter and strive to attend a workshop for a week. Continuing education keeps you sharp, in tune with current business trends, and may even land you a new client.

8. *Just Promote It.* Sales and promotion are every bit as important as being a good photographer. Let the editors that you want to work for know what you are doing. Show them images on a regular basis. Keep your name out there.

From "Business Tips for the Freelance Photographer," By Ira Gostin © 2003. Used with permission. To read this article in its entirety (highly recommended) go to: www.asmp.org/commerce/business_tips.php.

Appendix
Photography
Business Resources

They say you can never be too rich or too thin. While these could be argued, we say, "You can never have too many resources." Therefore, we present for your consideration a wealth of sources for you to check into, check out, and harness for your own personal information blitz.

These sources are tidbits, ideas to get you started on your research. They are by no means the only sources out there, and they should not be taken as the ultimate answer. We have done our research, but businesses do tend to move, change, fold, and expand. As we have repeatedly stressed, do your homework. Get out and start investigating.

Featured Photographers

Jerry Clement, Winter Springs, FL, www.clementfineartphotography. com

Carmen Davis, Carnation, WA, www.dogsinmotion.biz

Ira Gostin, Reno, NV, www.gostin.com

Ray Strawbridge, Bunn, NC, www.strawbridgephoto.com

Michael Weschler, New York City, NY, www.michaelweschler.com

▲

Photography Associations and Organizations

Advertising Photographers of America (APA), PO Box 250, White Plains, NY 10605, (800) 272-6264, fax (888) 889-7190, www.apanational.com

American Society of Media Photographers (ASMP), 150 North Second St., Philadelphia, PA 19106, (215) 451-2767, fax: (215) 451-0880, www.asmp.org

National Press Photographers Association (NPPA), 3200 Croasdaile Dr., Ste. 306, Durham, NC 27705, (919) 383-7246, fax: (919) 383-7261, www.nppa.org

North American Nature Photography Association (NANPA), 10200 West 44th Ave., Ste. 304, Wheat Ridge, CO 80033-2840, (303) 422-8527, fax: (303) 422-8894, www.nanpa.org

Picture Archive Council of America (PACA), (949) 282-5065, fax: (949) 282-5066, http://pacaoffice.org

Professional Photographers of America (PPA), 229 Peachtree St. NE, Ste. 2200, Atlanta, GA 30303, (800) 786-6277, fax: (404) 614-6400, www.ppa.com

Professional Women Photographers, 511 Avenue of the Americas, # 138, New York, NY 10011 www.pwponline.org

Special Kids Photography of America (SKPA), 1497 N. 775 West, Washington, UT 84780, (435) 627-1628 or (435) 632-8300, www.specialkidsphotography.com

Wedding Photojournalist Association (WPJA), www.wpja.org

Wedding & Portrait Photographers International (WPPI), PO Box 2003, 1312 Lincoln Boulevard, Santa Monica, CA USA 90406-2003, (310) 451-0090, fax: (310) 395-9058, www.wppionline.com

General Business Associations and Organizations

American Marketing Association, 311 S. Wacker Dr., #5800, Chicago, IL 60606, (800) AMA-1150, (312) 542-9000, fax: (312) 542-9001, www.marketingpower.com

Association of Small Business Development Centers, 8990 Burke Lake Rd., Burke, VA 22015, (703) 764-9850, fax: (703) 764-1234, www.asbdc-us.org

Business Networking International (BNI), 545 College Commerce Way, Upland, CA 91786 (800) 825-8286, www.bni.com

National Association of Women Business Owners, 8405 Greensboro Dr., Ste. #800, McLean, VA 22102, (800) 55-NAWBO, www.nawbo.org

National Association of Home Based Businesses (NAHBB), 10451 Mill Run Cir., Owings Mills, MD 21117, (410) 363-3698, www.usahomebusiness.com

Government Agencies and Related Resources

Department of Commerce, 1401 Constitution Ave. NW, Washington, DC 20230, (202) 482-2000, fax: (202) 482-5270, www.doc.gov

Department of Labor, 200 Constitution Ave. NW, Rm. S-1004, Washington, DC 20210, (866) 487-2365, (202) 219-6666, www.dol.gov

Federal Trade Commission, 600 Pennsylvania Ave. NW, Washington, DC 20580, (202) 326-2222, www.ftc.gov

IRS, 1111 Constitution Ave. NW, Washington, DC 20224, (202) 622-5000, www.irs.ustreas.gov

Library of Congress, Copyright Office, 101 Independence Ave. SE, Washington, DC 20559-6000, (202) 707-3000, www.loc.gov/copyright

SCORE, (national office), 409 Third St. SW, 6th Fl., Washington, DC 20024, (800) 634-0245, www.score.org

Small Business Administration, 409 Third St. SW, Washington, DC 20416, (800) 827-5722, www.sba.gov

U.S. Business Advisor, division of the Small Business Administration, www.business.gov

U.S. Patent and Trademark Office, Mail Stop USPTO Contact Center (UCC), PO Box 1450, Alexandria, VA 22313-1450, (800) 786-9199, fax: (571) 273-3245, www.uspto.gov

Books

American Society of Media Photographers, *ASMP Professional Business Practices in Photography* (Allworth Press; September, 2001)

Crawford, Tad, *Business and Legal Forms for Photographers* (with CD-ROM) (Allworth Press; January, 2002)

Fishman, Stephen, *Deduct It! Lower Your Small Business Taxes* (Nolo Press; November, 2006)

Heron, Michael and MacTavish, David, *Pricing Photography: The Complete Guide to Assignment & Stock Prices* (Allworth Press; January, 2002)

Leblanc, Mark, *Growing Your Business* (Expert Publishing, Inc.; September, 2003)

Lowell, Ross, *Matters of Light and Depth* (Lower Light Management; April, 1999)

Oppenheim, Selina, *Portfolios That Sell: Professional Techniques for Presenting and Marketing Your Photographs* (Amphoto Books; June, 2003)

Piscopo, Maria, *The Photographer's Guide to Marketing and Self-Promotion* (Allworth Press; July, 2001)

Poehner, Donna and O'Connell, Erika, *2007 Photographers Market* (Writers Digest Books; November 2006)

Tracy, Kathleen, *The Complete Idiot's Guide to Portrait Photography* (Alpha; June, 2002)

Magazines and Other Publications

Digital Photographer, c/o Miller Magazines Inc., 290 Maple Ct., Ste. 232, Ventura, CA 93003, www.digiphotomag.com

Entrepreneur, 2445 McCabe Way, Ste. 400, Irvine, CA 92614, (949) 261-2325, www.entrepreneur.com/magazine

PC World, 501 Second St., San Francisco CA 94107, (415) 243-0500, fax: (415) 442-1891, www.pcworld.com

Popular Photography and Imaging or *American Photo*, 1633 Broadway, New York, NY 10019, (212) 767-6000, fax: (212) 767-5602, www.popphoto.com

Professional Photographer, 229 Peachtree St. NE, Ste. 2200, International Tower, Atlanta, GA 30303, (404) 522-8600, ext. 260, fax: (404) 614-6406, www.ppmag.com

TradePub.com, free trade publications and white papers for small business owners, 16795 Lark Ave., Ste. 210, Los Gatos, CA 95032, (800) 882-4670, fax: (408) 884-1252, www.tradepub.com

Internet Resources

AltPick.com (Photographers Listing), 1123 Broadway, Ste. 716, New York, NY 10010, (212) 675-4176, fax: (212) 675-4403, www.altpick.com

Art Fair SourceBook (Guide to Art & Craft Fairs), 2003 NE 11th Ave., Portland, Oregon 97212-4027, (800) 358-2045, fax: (503) 331-0876, www.artfairsource.com

ArtSchools.com (Art School Directory), 3402 Route 8, Building D, Allison Park, PA 15101, (800) 940-0080, www.artschools.com

Double Exposure (for Digital Photographers), www.doubleexposure.com

PhotoLinks.ch (Photographers Listing), www.photolinks.ch

PhotoServe.com (Photographers Listing), www.photoserve.com

Salary.com, Compare salary ranges in your area with ranges in other parts of the country, www.salary.com

Stock Artists Alliance, http://stockartistsalliance.org

Sunshine Artist (Guide to Art Fairs & Festivals), 4075 L.B. McLeod Rd., Ste. E, Orlando, FL 32811, (407) 648-7479, www.sunshineartist.com

World Wide Learn (Online Degrees and Courses), 1501 17th Ave. SW, Ste. #150, Calgary, Alberta, T2T 0E2, (403) 802-6116, fax: (403) 802-6112, www.worldwidelearn.com

General Small Business Resources

BizFilings, information on incorporating and related services for business owners, including forms, advice, and tools needed, 8025 Excelsior Dr., Ste. 200, Madison, WI 53717, (800) 981-7183, (608) 827-5300, fax: (608) 827-5501, http://bizfilings.com

BPlans.com, free sample business plans, articles, and online tools, 144 E. 14th Ave., Eugene, OR 97401, (541) 683-6162, fax:(541) 683-6250, www.bplans.com

Business Finance.com, thousands of business loan and capital sources, 26741 Portola Parkway, Ste. 437, Foothill Ranch, CA 92610, (866) 892-9295, http://business-finance.com

Center for Business Planning, sample business plans and planning guidelines for business owners, 2013 Wells Branch Pkwy #206, Austin, Texas 78728, (512) 251-7541, fax: (512) 251-4401, http://businessplans.org

CCH Business Owner's Toolkit, provides customizable interactive forms and spread-sheets, plus other business tools and resources, www.toolkit.cch.com

Employers of America, information on writing job descriptions, HR manuals, safety tips, training resources, and more, PO Box 1874, Mason City, IA 50402-1874, (800) 728-3187 or (641) 424-3187, fax: 641-424-3187, www.employerhelp.org

Entrepreneur.com, tons of resources, guides, tips, articles and more at this informative web site for start-up businesses and growing companies, 2445 McCabe Way, Ste. 400, Irvine, CA 92614, (949) 261-2325, http://entrepreneur.com

The Entrepreneur Institute, provides resources and networking opportunities for business owners, 3592 Corporate Dr., Ste. 101, Columbus, OH 43231, (614) 895-1153, www.tei.net

Find Law for Small Business, links to regulatory agencies, sample forms and contracts, articles on all aspects of business development, 610 Opperman Dr., Egan, MN 55123, (651) 687-7000, fax: (800) 392-6206, http://smallbusiness.findlaw.com

Small Business Advisor, lots of articles and advice for start-up businesses, PO Box 579, Great Falls, VA 22066, (703) 450-7049, fax: (925) 226-4865, www.isquare.com

TeleCheck, provides check-guarantee services, 5251 Westheimer, Houston, TX 77056, (800) TELE-CHECK, www.telecheck.com

▲

WebSite Marketing Plan, lots of informative articles, as well as sample business and marketing plans, 8050 Watson Rd., Ste. 315, St. Louis, MO 63119, www.websitemarketingplan.com

Franchise and Business Opportunities

The American Franchisee Association, 53 West Jackson Blvd, Ste. 1157, Chicago, IL 60604, (312) 431-0545, fax: (312) 431-1469, www.franchisee.org

BizBuySell, useful web site to find businesses for sale as well as online tools and articles, 185 Berry St., Ste. 4000, San Francisco, CA 94107, (415) 284-4380, fax: (415) 764-1622, http://bizbuysell.com

Franchise Direct, (888) 712-1994, (800) 719-0296, www.franchisedirect.com

Franchise Gator, 599 W. Crossville Rd., Roswell, GA 30075, (678) 748-3000, www.franchisegator.com

International Franchise Association, 1350 New York Ave. NW, #900, Washington, DC 20005-4709, (202) 628-8000, fax: (202) 628-0812, www.franchise.org

Trade Shows and Meetings

Specialty Trade Shows, 3939 Hardie Rd., Coconut Grove, FL 33133-6437, (305) 663-6635, fax: (305) 661-8118, www.spectrade.com

Tradeshow Week, 5700 Wilshire Blvd., #120, Los Angeles, CA 90036-5804, www.tradeshowweek.com

Tradeshow News Network, 1904 Vintage Dr., Corinth, TX 76210, (972) 504-6358, (972) 321-3705, www.tsnn.com

Glossary

All rights: the unrestricted right to reproduce, distribute, display, and perform an image; not a copyright transfer

Ambient light: the available light surrounding a subject; illumination not provided by the photographer

Analog: a/k/a traditional film camera

Aperture: circular opening in a lens that admits light

Assignment: agreement to produce photographic images according to client specifications, to be used only in the manner described by a grant of usage rights

Autofocus: device that is used to automatically focus an image in cameras, projectors, and enlargers

Background: area shown behind the main subject in a picture

Bid: legally binding proposal formulated by photographer based on scope of project description

Box camera: introduced by George Eastman in 1888, the most uncomplicated camera invented

Cable release: flexible cable used for closing a camera shutter hands-free

Candid pictures: unposed pictures of people and animals, often taken without the subject's knowledge.

Cibachrome: rarely used color printing process that produces color prints directly from color slides; now called Ilfochrome

Copyright: given to the legal owner of a particular photograph or piece of work

Copyright infringement: act of violating a copyright owner's exclusive rights

Daguerreotype: first practical photographic process, introduced by Louis Daguerre in 1839

Darkroom: room where natural light is excluded so that images can be developed and printed using light-sensitive materials.

Day rate: pre-agreed, flat-rate fee paid for up to one day of production work

Embargo period: a period of time during which an image may not be licensed, published, and/or distributed

Enlarger: device for producing prints by projecting an enlarged image on sensitive paper

Estimate: an approximation of fees and costs formulated by photographer based on scope of project description; non-binding

Film: a coated strip for taking pictures on a flexible, transparent base that records images or scenes.

Filters: colored glass, gelatin, or plastic disks, used to modify the light passing through them, mainly in terms of color content

Flash: brief, bright illumination caused by an artificial light source

Flat: used to describe a negative or print with very low contrast

Image: a likeness of a real object or person, produced electronically, through a lens, or in a picture

Kelvin: unit of absolute temperature

Lens: optical device made of glass or plastic and capable of bending and focusing light

Lightbox: box of fluorescent light used for viewing, registering, or correcting film negatives and positives

Mat: a cardboard rectangle with an opening cut in it that is placed over a print to frame it

Negative: film that produces an image by the product of exposure and development, in which tones are reversed so that highlights appear dark and shadows appear light

Positive: the production of prints or transparencies in which light and dark correspond to the tonal range of the subject

Print: a photographic image on paper

Shutter: camera device that controls the duration of the exposure by opening and closing the lens aperture

Slide: photographic transparency mounted for projection to produce an image

Still life: inanimate subject arranged to make full use of form, shape, and lighting

Subject: person or thing photographed

Tripod: three-legged camera support that can usually be height adjusted

Index